# Heaven Bound

## What You Need To Know About
## The Journey of Your Lifetime

**Dr. Edwin F. Jenkins**

with Andrew Edwin Jenkins

*Heaven Bound: What You Need to Know About the Journey of Your Lifetime*

Copyright, 2023, Dr. Edwin F. Jenkins

Unless otherwise noted…

For more information, go to www.LifeLift.online

# Contents

## Part 4 — What Will We Do?

## Resources

Register for free access at LifeLift.online/1

**Claim your free audiobook**

# Introduction

Somebody once said that we can "become so Heavenly-minded that we're no earthly good."

Turns out, the opposite is true. **Being Heavenly-minded is good for every area of life.** Remembering our ultimate destination (as well as our most important citizenship) empowers us to think long-term, to endure difficult seasons, and to live for the things that matter most.

But it's hard to be Heavenly-minded when you don't know much about the place. (And, there aren't many books, sermons, and studies on the subject, even though the Bible is a treasure-trove of truths about our eternal Home.)

**In *Heaven Bound*, you'll learn what you need to know about the literal journey of your lifetime.** In the process, we'll—

- Talk about what Heaven is actually like— and how the "present Heaven" (where people go when they die) differs from the "permanent Heaven" (where we'll be forever)

- Take a closer look at some of the important themes in Scripture that we don't pay much attention to— including why the physical Resurrection of Jesus practically matters

- Tackle 18 common questions about Heaven, including what you'll look like, what personality and age you'll have, whether or not you'll still be married, and if we'll be spirits or actual people— and if Heaven will be physical or not

- Test commonly held beliefs about Heaven against the truth of Scripture (and identify a few major misconceptions— false beliefs held even in the Church)

- Travel back in time to see how brothers and sisters in Christ felt their certainty of Heaven empowered them to fill their years on earth with significance

This study is sub-divided into four parts. We'll explore:

1. What Heaven is (Part 1)

2. Biblical truths we need to study more often— as they relate to Heaven specifically (Part 2)

3. What life in Heaven is like (Part 3)

4. What we'll do when we get there (Part 4)

And, we've provided a teaching outline in the appendix, should you choose to share this information with others, lead a group, or just take a deeper dive on your own.

In the same way that we prepare for vacations and holidays based on where we're headed, so also should we prepare for Heaven. The destination informs the journey. Prepare to enjoy the journey of your lifetime.

# Heaven Bound

# Overview

The main idea for each chapter is provided here to offer an overview of where we're headed in our study.

## Part 1 — What is Heaven?

### 1. Being Heavenly-Minded is Earthly Good

*Main idea: The destination you plan to reach informs your journey— including how you plan and prepare during the days leading to your arrival. Likewise, being heavenly-minded is earthly good.*

### 2. The Difference in Heaven Now & Heaven in the Future

*Main idea: The present Heaven provides us a glimpse of the future Heaven. The present Heaven is where believers go when they die— and is the sacred place many have seen.*

### 3. The Essence of Eternal Life

*Main idea: Jesus defined eternal life as "knowing God." In Heaven we will be fully present with all of God, yet we will also continue receiving unfolding revelation of His goodness and glory.*

## Part 2 — Truths to Think About More Often

### 4. Why the Resurrection Means So Much

*Main idea: When Jesus arose from the dead 2,000 years ago, we arose with Him. Furthermore, He became the first fruits of the New Creation, showing what we're destined to become.*

### 5. Our Role in Ruling with Christ

*Main idea: From the beginning of time, we discover that we were created for relationship and rulership. Although the Fall postponed our potential, it didn't eliminate— or change— it.*

### 6. Understanding the Millennium

*Main idea: Though there is some disagreement as to when the reign occurs and whether the 1,000 years is symbolic or literal, we can all agree: Jesus returns and reigns. Moreover, we will see a radical difference between His first coming and His return.*

## Part 3 — What Will Heaven Be Like?

### 7. The Old Passes (the New Heaven and the New Earth)

*Main idea: A New Heaven and a New Earth are coming— they're promised. Before they can arrive, though, the present Earth must pass.*

### 8. The New Comes (the New Heaven and the New Earth)

*Main idea: Scripture describes the New Heaven and New Earth— what is coming — as both a country and a city. This is the place of our true citizenship.*

### 9. Life in Heaven

*Main idea: Heaven is our permanent home. And, though questions abound, we can take comfort in the fact that God is completely good and He has prepared Heaven with us in mind.*

## Part 4 — What Will We Do?

## 10. Destined for Deeper Relationships

*Main idea: God is relational, and we're created in His image. We were, therefore, designed for relationship— with Him and with others. In Heaven this won't be lessened; it will be amplified.*

## 11. Managing the Misconceptions and Clarifying Expectations

*Main idea: Since we study Heaven so little, misconceptions abound. However, Heaven will be the most fulfilling experience— and it won't end. In fact, it will continue getting better and better the longer it lasts.*

## 12. Worship as a Way of Life— Then and Now

*Main idea: Worship will be our way of life in Heaven (our definition of worship is far too narrow). We began our study learning about how to plan for our ultimate destination. One of the best ways to prepare is to live now in the same way we'll live then— with worship as our way of life, living the prayer "on earth as it is in Heaven."*

14

# Part 1 — What is Heaven?

# 1. Being Heavenly-Minded is Earthly Good

---

**Main idea: The destination you plan to reach informs your journey— including how you plan and prepare during the days leading to your arrival. Likewise, being heavenly-minded is earthly good.**

---

*The man who is about to sail for Australia or New Zealand as a settler, is naturally anxious to know something about his future home, its climate, its employments, its inhabitants, its ways, its customs. All these are subjects of deep interest to him. You are leaving the land of your nativity, you are going to spend the rest of your life in a new hemisphere. It would be strange indeed if you did not desire information about your new abode.*

*Now surely, if we hope to dwell forever in that "better country, even a heavenly one," we ought to seek all the knowledge we can get about it. Before we go to our eternal home we should try to become acquainted with it.*

*— J.C. Ryle*[1]

---

[1] Quoted by Randy Alcorn in *Heaven*, page 5.

# A. Planning the journey for a place you have never been

Do you seek to find out at least some things about the destination that might be helpful to know before you arrive? Things like where the destination is located, how to get there, what might be expected upon arrival and what activities might involve you after your arrival?

How long may you expect to stay and what accommodations should you expect to find? Are there any required documents which should be prepared?

Do you know any other persons who are making or have made a similar trip? Whom should you expect to see? Will you be involved with anyone you have known before or will all persons who are at the destination be new to you? How many other people will be there?

1.  **Have we actually neglected to carefully consider what the Bible says about Heaven, our ultimate destination?**

    John Eldridge, in his book the *Journey of Desire,* expresses what many people seem to believe about Heaven.[2]

    *Nearly every Christian I have spoken with has some idea that eternity is an un-ending church service….*

    *We have settled on an image of the never-ending sing-along in the sky, one great hymn after another, forever and ever, amen. And our heart sinks.*

    *Forever and ever?*

    *That's it?*

---

[2] Quoted by Randy Alcorn in his book *Heaven.*

*That's the good news?*

*And then we sigh and feel guilty that we are not more "spiritual." We lose heart and we turn once more to the present to find what life we can.*


2. **What do you personally believe about Heaven?**

What people believe about Heaven varies widely.

_____

_____

_____


3. **Why do you think there has there been so much neglect regarding teaching and learning about Heaven?**

Consider the following two verses, John 8:44 and Revelation 13:6.

John 8:44—

*You belong to your father, the devil, and you want to carry out your father's desires. He was a murderer from the beginning, not holding to the truth, for there is no truth in him. When he lies, he speaks his native language, for he is a liar and the father of lies.*

Revelation 13:6—

*It opened its mouth to blaspheme God, and to slander his name and his dwelling place and those who live in heaven.*

Satan and the satanic beast of Revelation lie and slander basically three things:

1. **God's Person** (who He is and what He is like)

2. **God's People** (who we are, how we are loved by Him, our identity)

3. **God's Place** (Heaven)

Most of us realize we live on a battlefield. Our ultimate enemy (though already defeated) seems unconvinced. Yet, we can find ourselves as unwitting contributors to his ongoing warfare activities.

Satan's strategy seems evident: question God's truthfulness and convince us that God's future plans for us are boring, sad, and undesirable.

H.G. Wells tells the story of a tribe in a remote valley deep in a towering mountain range. There was a terrible epidemic in which all of the villagers lost their sight. Generations came with no awareness of sight, a world unable to see who did not know their condition.[3]

Randy Alcorn declares that, spiritually speaking, we live in the "country of the blind."

During seminary I served with a pastor who many characterized as "clueless." My friend never realized he was "clueless," but lived his life with unique joy and gladness.

The disease of sin, carnality, and earthliness blinds to what lies beyond and the possibility of that which is better— and more fulfilling. Jesus came to show us more, to make possible the abundant life-relationship. **The more we learn about His intention and preparation for us, the better off we will be right now.**

---

[3] Randy Alcorn, *Heaven*, page 11 cites H.G. Wells, *The Country of the Blind.*

## B. Look up!

**What difference could and should an accurate belief about Heaven have on my life now and in the future?**

Most of us have heard the comment "he or she is so heavenly-minded that he or she is no earthly good."

**What does that statement mean?**

**How does that statement measure up with Colossians 3:1-4?**

Colossians 3:1-4—

> Since, then, you have been raised with Christ, **set your hearts on things above, where Christ is, seated at the right hand of God. Set your minds on things above, not on earthly things.** For you died, and your life is now hidden with Christ in God. When Christ, who is your life, appears, then you also will appear with him in glory.

Notice what C.S. Lewis penned in his book *Mere Christianity*.

> If you read history, you will find that the **Christians who did most for the present world were just those who thought most of the next.** The Apostles themselves, who set on foot the conversion of the Roman Empire, the great men who built up the Middle Ages, English Evangelicals who abolished the Slave Trade, all left their mark on Earth, precisely because their minds were occupied with Heaven. It is since Christians have largely ceased to think of the other world that they have become so ineffective in this.
>
> **Aim at Heaven and you will get earth "thrown in": aim at earth and you will get neither.**

## C. Four earthly benefits of being Heavenly-minded

**Certain benefits may be expected for the "Heavenly minded."** Consider these four.

1. **Focusing on Heaven reminds us of the brevity of our earthly life.**

   Bruce Wilkinson—

   *"Everything you do today matters forever."*

   Randy Alcorn—

   *"As human beings, we have a terminal disease called mortality."*

   How long do you expect to live on this earth?

   Suppose that time is briefer than you expect?

   Suppose that time is longer than you expect?

   What about the backdrop of eternity?

   _____

   _____

   _____

   Notice the Biblical perspective from these four passages:

   James 4:14—

*Why, you do not even know what will happen tomorrow. What is your life?* **You are a mist that appears for a little while and then vanishes.**

1 Peter 1:24—

**All people are like grass,** *and all their glory is like the flowers of the field; the grass withers and the flowers fall…*

Psalm 39:1-5—

*I said, "I will watch my ways and keep my tongue from sin; I will put a muzzle on my mouth while in the presence of the wicked."*

*So I remained utterly silent, not even saying anything good.*

*But my anguish increased; my heart grew hot within me.*

*While I meditated, the fire burned; then I spoke with my tongue:* **"Show me, Lord, my life's end and the number of my days; let me know how fleeting my life is."**

*You have made my days a mere handbreadth; the span of my years is as nothing before you.*

*Everyone is but a breath, even those who seem secure.*

Psalm 90:4,10,12—

*A thousand years in your sight are like a day that has just gone by, or like a watch in the night.*

*Our days may come to seventy years, or eighty, if our strength endures; yet the best of them are but trouble and sorrow.*

**Teach us to number our days, that we may gain a heart of wisdom.**

Consider the story of Florence Chadwick…

Florence had swum the English Channel two times before she began an arduous swim in the Pacific Ocean from Catalina Island to the mainland.

After swimming for 15 hours in the foggy, chilly water Florence could hardly see the boats that were accompanying her. Florence's mother was in one of the boats. Florence begged to be taken out of the water.

Urged on that she could make it, she continued her swim.

Finally, physically and emotionally exhausted Florence stopped swimming and was pulled out. Aboard the ship she discovered the shore lay only a half mile away.

She said, "All I could see was the fog... I think if I have seen the shore, I would have made it."

We must keep our signs on Jesus, the Rock of Salvation.

## 2. Focusing on Heaven prepares us for the certainty of judgment.

Earth is a training ground for Heaven.

We need to understand that we will give account and be rewarded for the way in which we have followed the directives of our Lord Jesus.

Notice these four additional passages:

Matthew 7:13-14—

*Enter through the narrow gate. For wide is the gate and broad is the road that leads to destruction, and many enter through it.*

*But small is the gate and narrow the road that leads to life, and only a few find it.*

Hebrews 9:27—

*Just as people are destined to die once, and **after that to face judgment...***

2 Corinthians 5:10—

**For we must all appear before the judgment seat of Christ**, *so that each of us may receive what is due us for the things done while in the body, whether good or bad.*

Revelation 20:11-15—

*Then I saw a great white throne and him who was seated on it. The earth and the heavens fled from his presence, and there was no place for them.*

*And I saw the dead, great and small, standing before the throne, and books were opened. Another book was opened, which is the book of life. **The dead were judged according to what they had done as recorded in the books.***

*The sea gave up the dead that were in it, and death and Hades gave up the dead that were in them, and each person was judged according to what they had done.*

*Then death and Hades were thrown into the lake of fire. The lake of fire is the second death. Anyone whose name was not found written in the book of life was thrown into the lake of fire.*

## 3. Focusing on Heaven motivates us to live pure lives.

We live in a world that seems to have lost its way.

Because we have found The Way, The Truth and The Life in Jesus Christ, we ought to so live that the world may see Christ living in and working through us.

Consider these three passages.

1 Corinthians 3:13—

> … *their work will be shown for what it is, because the Day will bring it to light. It will be revealed with fire, and* **the fire will test the quality of each person's work.**

1 John 3:2-3—

> *Dear friends, now we are children of God, and what we will be has not yet been made known. But we know that when Christ appears, we shall be like him, for we shall see him as he is.* **All who have this hope in him purify themselves, just as he is pure.**

Philippians 3:9-10—

> … *and be found in him, not having a righteousness of my own that comes from the law, but that which is through faith in Christ—the righteousness that comes from God on the basis of faith.*
>
> *I want to know Christ—yes, to know the power of his resurrection and participation in his sufferings, becoming like him in his death.*

## 4. Focusing on Heaven places suffering in perspective.

The problems of this life that have come as a result of the Curse will not be set right until Christ returns and sets up his Kingdom. In the meantime, we should joyfully endure faithfully anticipating that glorious time.

Reflect on the following—

2 Corinthians 4:17-18—

> **For our light and momentary troubles are achieving for us an eternal glory that far outweighs them all.** *So we fix our eyes not*

*on what is seen, but on what is unseen, since what is seen is temporary, but what is unseen is eternal.*

Romans 8:19-25—

*For the creation waits in eager expectation for the children of God to be revealed. For the creation was subjected to frustration, not by its own choice, but by the will of the one who subjected it, in hope that the creation itself will be liberated from its bondage to decay and brought into the freedom and glory of the children of God.*

*We know that the whole creation has been groaning as in the pains of childbirth right up to the present time.* **Not only so, but we ourselves, who have the first fruits of the Spirit, groan inwardly as we wait eagerly for our adoption to sonship, the redemption of our bodies.**

*For in this hope we were saved. But hope that is seen is no hope at all. Who hopes for what they already have?*

*But if we hope for what we do not yet have,* **we wait for it patiently.**

# 4 BENEFITS OF BEING HEAVENLY-MINDED

1. Brevity of life

2. Certainty of judgement

3. Motivation to live pure

4. Perspective when suffering

## D. How can we "know" if we haven't seen it?

**Since focusing on Heaven is so beneficial, how can we hope to know about Heaven if "no eye has seen"?**

Even the things we haven't seen physically, God has shown us spiritually:

1 Corinthians 2:9-10—

> However, as it is written: "What no eye has seen, what no ear has heard, and what no human mind has conceived"— **the things God has prepared for those who love Him— these are the things God has revealed to us by His Spirit.**

Randy Alcorn answers this concern in an extremely helpful manner:

> What we otherwise could not have known about Heaven, because we're unable to see it, God says He has revealed to us through his Spirit.
>
> This means that God has explained to us what Heaven is like. Not exhaustively, but accurately.
>
> God tells us about Heaven in His Word, not so we can shrug our shoulders and remain ignorant, but because He wants us to understand and anticipate what awaits us.[4]

Another verse of great importance to us is Deuteronomy 29:29. Again, we must be sure to read the entire verse.

Deuteronomy 29:29—

> The secret things belong to the Lord our God, but **the things revealed belong to us and to our children forever, that we may follow all the words of this law**.

---

[4] *Heaven*, page 19.

## E. How, then, should we prepare?

**Based on these things as we embark on our journey to learn about our ultimate destination, what do we need to do right now?**

1. **Be sincerely grateful for our Heavenly citizenship.**

   Philippians 3:20-21—

   > **But our citizenship is in heaven.** *And we eagerly await a Savior from there, the Lord Jesus Christ, who, by the power that enables him to bring everything under his control, will transform our lowly bodies so that they will be like his glorious body.*

2. **Focus our thinking on the things above to develop an eternal perspective.**

   Colossians 3:1-2—

   > *Since, then, you have been raised with Christ, set your hearts on things above, where Christ is, seated at the right hand of God.* ***Set your minds on things above, not on earthly things.***

3. **Remember we are pressing forward toward the prize prepared for us.**

   Philippians 3:13-14—

   > *Brothers and sisters, I do not consider myself yet to have taken hold of it.*

*But one thing I do: Forgetting what is behind and straining toward what is ahead, **I press on toward the goal to win the prize for which God has called me heavenward in Christ Jesus**.*

*PREPARING FOR OUR JOURNEY*

# 1. BE GRATEFUL
— YOU'RE A CITIZEN OF HEAVEN

# 2. FOCUS
— ON THE THINGS OF HEAVEN

# 3. PRESS ON
— STAND FAST ON THE JOURNEY

## When We All Get to Heaven

*Sing the wondrous love of Jesus,*
*Sing His mercy and His grace;*
*In the mansions bright and blessed*
*He'll prepare for us a place.*

*When we all get to Heaven,*
*What a day of rejoicing that will be!*
*When we all see Jesus,*
*We'll sing and shout the victory!*

*While we walk the pilgrim pathway,*
*Clouds will overspread the sky;*
*But when trav'ling days are over,*
*Not a shadow, not a sigh.*

*Let us then be true and faithful,*
*Trusting, serving every day;*
*Just one glimpse of Him in glory*
*Will the toils of life repay.*

*Onward to the prize before us!*
*Soon His beauty we'll behold;*
*Soon the pearly gates will open;*
*We shall tread the streets of gold.*

*—Thomas Mosie Lister*

# 1. Being Heavenly-Minded is Earthly Good

32

# 2. The Difference in Heaven Now & Heaven in the Future

---

**Main idea: The present Heaven provides us a glimpse of the future Heaven. The present Heaven is where believers go when they die— and is the sacred place many have seen.**

---

*It bears repeating because it is so commonly misunderstood: When we die, believers in Christ will not go to Heaven where we'll live forever. Instead, we'll go to an intermediate Heaven.*

*In that Heaven— where those who died covered by Christ's blood are now— we'll await the time of Christ's return to the earth, our bodily resurrection, the final judgment, and the creation of the new heavens and the New Earth.*

*If we fail to grasp this truth, we will fail to understand the biblical doctrine of Heaven.*

*— Randy Alcorn*[5]

Questions and answers can help us understand more about Heaven— such as:

- What is the nature of the "present Heaven"?

---

[5] *Heaven*, page 42

• Is the "present Heaven" a part of our universe or another?

# A. According to theologians the Bible actually refers to multiple "heavens."

1. **The 1st heaven is Earth's atmosphere.**

   The 1st heaven is where we live and breathe and birds and airplanes fly.

2. **The 2nd heaven is what we usually call outer space.**

   This is where the planets, stars, and millions of galaxies are present in this vast universe.

3. **The 3rd Heaven points to the place where God dwells.**

   The presence of God is the most prominent feature.

   All Christians go immediately to this Heaven at the time of death. This is what is meant by the fact that to be absent from the body is to be present with the Lord.

   2 Corinthians 5:6-8—

   > *Therefore we are always confident and know that as long as we are at home in the body we are away from the Lord. For we live by faith, not by sight. We are confident, I say, and would prefer to be **away from the body and at home with the Lord.***

Also, Paul writes about being caught up into this 3rd heaven.

2 Corinthians 12:3-4—

*And I know that this man—whether in the body or apart from the body I do not know, but God knows, was caught up to paradise and heard inexpressible things, things that no one is permitted to tell.*

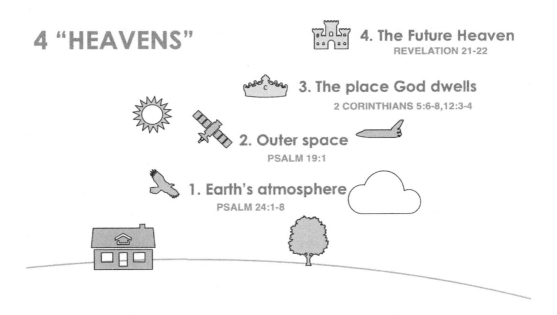

# 4 "HEAVENS"

**4. The Future Heaven**
REVELATION 21-22

**3. The place God dwells**
2 CORINTHIANS 5:6-8,12:3-4

**2. Outer space**
PSALM 19:1

**1. Earth's atmosphere**
PSALM 24:1-8

4. **The 4th Heaven refers to a future Heaven that God is preparing for us even now.**

This is to be the place of our forever home. It is a geographical location that includes the New Heaven and the New Earth and the New Jerusalem.

Revelation 21-22 speaks of this 4th Heaven.

Revelation 21:1-2, 21:22-23—

> Then I saw "a new heaven and a new earth," for the first heaven and the first earth had passed away, and there was no longer any sea.
>
> I saw the Holy City, the new Jerusalem, coming down out of heaven from God, prepared as a bride beautifully dressed for her husband.
>
> I did not see a temple in the city, because the Lord God Almighty and the Lamb are its temple. The city does not need the sun or the moon to shine on it, for the glory of God gives it light, and the Lamb is its lamp.

# B. Understanding the present Heaven and the future Heaven

**At some time in the future, the present Heaven—where God, Angels, and believers who have died are now— will be combined with the future Heaven.**

This will be known as the New Heaven, the New Earth, the New Jerusalem. This will happen after the rapture, Judgment seat of Christ, the seven-year tribulation, the battle of Armageddon, the Millennial Kingdom, and the Great White Throne Judgment.

In his book about Heaven, Paul Enns points to the following Scriptures that indicate Heaven is— right now— a different realm that is, concurrently, near to us.

Read these eleven passages which highlight the nearness of the present Heaven to life right now—

1. **Elisha saw Elijah go up into Heaven by a whirlwind.**

2 Kings 2:11—

*As they were walking along and talking together, suddenly a chariot of fire and horses of fire appeared and separated the two of them, and Elijah went up to heaven in a whirlwind.*

2.  **Isaiah saw the Lord on His throne.**

Isaiah 6:1-5—

*In the year that King Uzziah died, I saw the Lord, high and exalted, seated on a throne; and the train of his robe filled the temple. Above him were seraphim, each with six wings: With two wings they covered their faces, with two they covered their feet, and with two they were flying.*

*And they were calling to one another: "Holy, holy, holy is the Lord Almighty; the whole earth is full of his glory."*

*At the sound of their voices the doorposts and thresholds shook and the temple was filled with smoke.*

*"Woe to me!" I cried. "I am ruined! For I am a man of unclean lips, and I live among a people of unclean lips, and my eyes have seen the King, the Lord Almighty."*

3.  **Ezekiel saw visions of God in the Heavenly throne room.**

Ezekiel 1:1—

*In my thirtieth year, in the fourth month on the fifth day, while I was among the exiles by the Kebar River, the heavens were opened and I saw visions of God.*

4.   **Nebuchadnezzar saw visions of Heaven.**

   Daniel 4:13,23,31—

   *In the visions I saw while lying in bed, I looked, and there before me was a holy one, a messenger, coming down from Heaven…*

   *Your Majesty saw a holy one, a messenger, coming down from Heaven and saying, "Cut down the tree and destroy it, but leave the stump, bound with iron and bronze, in the grass of the field, while its roots remain in the ground. Let him be drenched with the dew of heaven; let him live with the wild animals, until seven times pass by for him."*

   *…Even as the words were on his lips, a voice came from heaven, "This is what is decreed for you, King Nebuchadnezzar: Your royal authority has been taken from you."*

5.   **Daniel saw into Heaven in the night visions.**

   Daniel 7:13—

   *In my vision at night I looked, and there before me was one like a son of man, coming with the clouds of heaven. He approached the Ancient of Days and was led into his presence.*

6.   **Stephen saw Jesus Standing at the right hand of God.**

   Acts 7:55-56—

   *But Stephen, full of the Holy Spirit, looked up to heaven and saw the glory of God, and Jesus standing at the right hand of God.*

   *"Look," he said, "I see heaven open and the Son of Man standing at the right hand of God."*

7. **Paul heard Jesus speaking to him from Heaven.**

   Acts 9:3-4—

   *As he neared Damascus on his journey, suddenly a light from heaven flashed around him. He fell to the ground and heard a voice say to him, "Saul, Saul, why do you persecute me?"*


8. **Peter talked with the Lord.**

   Acts 10:10-11—

   *He became hungry and wanted something to eat, and while the meal was being prepared, he fell into a trance. He saw heaven opened and something like a large sheet being let down to earth by its four corners.*


9. **John saw an angel and heard a great multitude from Heaven.**

   Revelation 18:1,19:1—

   *After this I saw another angel coming down from heaven. He had great authority, and the earth was illuminated by his splendor…*

   *After this I heard what sounded like the roar of a great multitude in heaven shouting…*


10. **Jesus told Nathanael that he would see Heaven opened.**

    John 1:51—

    *He then added, "Very truly I tell you, you will see heaven open, and the angels of God ascending and descending on the Son of Man."*

**11. Jesus saw the Heavens opened and the Spirit of God descending.**

Matthew 3:16—

> *As soon as Jesus was baptized, he went up out of the water. At that moment heaven was opened, and he saw the Spirit of God descending like a dove and alighting on him.*

Again, the Scriptures indicate the nearness of Heaven to us in another realm.

# C. Where do believers in Jesus Christ go when they die?

Heaven is presented in several ways in the Scriptures— as a Garden, a City, a Country, and a Kingdom.

However we envision it, we know this: the place where believers go *now* is the "Present Heaven" or "Intermediate Heaven."

The Present Heaven / Intermediate Heaven—

- It is not a partial Heaven or something second-rate.

- It is fully Heaven and completely in God's presence.

However, at the same time, God is preparing a forever Heaven that follows the Resurrection and may be spoken of as the New Heaven and the New Earth spoken of in Scripture.

Revelation 21:1-4—

> *Then **I saw "a new heaven and a new earth," for the first heaven and the first earth had passed away**, and there was no longer any sea.*

*I saw the Holy City, the new Jerusalem, coming down out of heaven from God, prepared as a bride beautifully dressed for her husband.*

*And I heard a loud voice from the throne saying, "Look! God's dwelling place is now among the people, and he will dwell with them. They will be his people, and God himself will be with them and be their God. He will wipe every tear from their eyes. There will be no more death or mourning or crying or pain, for the old order of things has passed away."*

## Primary Differences

| PRESENT HEAVEN | FUTURE HEAVEN |
| --- | --- |
| Is the place believers go when they die | Is the place we all go after the "dead in Christ" rise and those who are alive meet them. |
| Has been seen by many— note the referenced Biblical passages | "No eye hath seen…" |
| Is prepared for us (i.e., "Today, you will be with Me in Paradise.) | Is being prepared ("I go prepare a place for you…") |

**A few aspects of the Future Heaven—**

- The New Earth will be like Eden.

- The Tree of Life will be on Earth.

- The River of Life will flow forever.

- The deserts will gush with water.

- A beautiful and bountiful land will flourish.

- Animals will be plentiful and peaceful.

Notice the following verses—

Isaiah 30:23b-24—

> In that day your cattle will graze in broad meadows. The oxen and donkeys that work the soil will eat fodder and mash, spread out with fork and shovel.

Isaiah 61:5—

> Strangers will shepherd your flocks; foreigners will work your fields and vineyards.

Isaiah 11:6-9a—

> The wolf will live with the lamb,
> the leopard will lie down with the goat,
> the calf and the lion and the yearling together;
> and a little child will lead them.
> The cow will feed with the bear,
> their young will lie down together,
> and the lion will eat straw like the ox.
> The infant will play near the cobra's den,
> and the young child will put its hand into the viper's nest.
> They will neither harm nor destroy on all my holy mountain.

Isaiah 32:20—

> ... how blessed you will be, sowing your seed by every stream.

Dr. Wayne Grudem says the following about Heaven.[6]

> *Christians often talk about living with God "in Heaven" forever. But, in fact, the Biblical teaching is richer than that: it tells us there will be new heavens and a new earth— an entirely renewed creation--- and we will live with God there…*
>
> *There will also be a new kind of unification of Heaven and earth...*
>
> *There will be a joining of Heaven and earth in this new creation.*

**GETTING CLARITY**

*WE OFTEN ASSUME THINGS THAT AREN'T ACCURATE ABOUT HEAVEN*

| Assumptions | Accurate |
|---|---|
| Non-earth | New Earth |
| Unfamiliar, otherworldly | Familiar, earthly |
| Disembodied | Resurrected |
| Foreign | Home |
| Leave things behind | Best things ahead |
| Static | Dynamic |
| Strange, unknown | Both old & new |
| Nothing to do | God to worship & serve |
| No learning or discovery | Ongoing discovery |
| Boring | Fascinating |
| Loss of desire | Fulfillment of desire |
| Absence of the terrible | Presence of the wonderful |

# D. Is the "Present Heaven" a physical place?

We have several assumptions about Heaven that, though well-intended, fall flat compared to the portrait painted by Scripture. Write some assumptions that you've heard or that you have thought or at least wondered about.

---

6 Quoted by Randy Alcorn, in his book *Heaven*, page 42.

_____

_____

Ecclesiastes 12:7—

*... and the dust returns to the ground it came from, and the spirit returns to God who gave it.*

Luke 16:22-31—

*The time came when the beggar died and the angels carried him to Abraham's side. The rich man also died and was buried. In Hades, where he was in torment, he looked up and saw Abraham far away, with Lazarus by his side.*

*So he called to him, "Father Abraham, have pity on me and send Lazarus to dip the tip of his finger in water and cool my tongue, because I am in agony in this fire."*

*But Abraham replied, "Son, remember that in your lifetime you received your good things, while Lazarus received bad things, but now he is comforted here and you are in agony. And besides all this, between us and you a great chasm has been set in place, so that those who want to go from here to you cannot, nor can anyone cross over from there to us."*

*He answered, "Then I beg you, father, send Lazarus to my family, for I have five brothers. Let him warn them, so that they will not also come to this place of torment."*

*Abraham replied, "They have Moses and the Prophets; let them listen to them."*

*"No, father Abraham," he said, "but if someone from the dead goes to them, they will repent."*

*He said to him, "If they do not listen to Moses and the Prophets, they will not be convinced even if someone rises from the dead."*

Luke 23:43—

*Jesus answered him, "Truly I tell you, **today you will be with me in paradise**."*

Acts 7:55-56—

*But Stephen, full of the Holy Spirit, **looked up to heaven and saw the glory of God, and Jesus standing at the right hand of God**.*

*"Look," he said, "**I see heaven open** and the Son of Man standing at the right hand of God."*

Philippians 1:23-24—

*I am torn between the two: **I desire to depart and be with Christ**, which is better by far; but it is more necessary for you that I remain in the body.*

2 Corinthians 5:6-8—

*Therefore we are always confident and know that as long as we are at home in the body we are away from the Lord. For we live by faith, not by sight.*

*We are confident, I say, and would **prefer to be away from the body and at home with the Lord**.*

# E. How we might understand it— a helpful "parable."

Randy Alcorn shares a helpful illustration of the difference between the present Heaven and the future Heaven.[7] With several added thoughts, here is his idea:

---

[7] See his book *Heaven* for more, page 43.

*Suppose you are living in a homeless shelter in Miami. You inherit a beautiful house in Santa Barbara, California.*

*You will fly to Santa Barbara to receive ownership of your new house. Other family members and friends who moved from Miami years ago will be there near where you will live in a remarkable setting and place designed especially for you. You are assured of an exciting, fruitful, fulfilling, and marvelous future.*

*On the way you change planes in Denver, having a temporary but extremely enjoyable stopover. You meet and enjoy a remarkable time with the benefactor and provider of your inheritance.*

*He will also be in Santa Barbara when you arrive there.*

*You also come into contact with others who will be going on to Santa Barbara, as well.*

*If someone you meet asks you where you are going you would say Santa Barbara because that is your ultimate destination. However, you will stop off in Denver which is a temporary stop off before you and your fellow passengers reach your final destination, Santa Barbara.*

# 3. The Essence of Eternal Life

---

**Main idea: Jesus defined eternal life as "knowing God." In Heaven we will be fully present with all of God, yet we will also continue receiving unfolding revelation of His goodness and glory.**

---

*The Old Testament reports that though they were chosen by God, the people of Israel could not approach God physically. God's presence was a frightening phenomenon, evidenced by thunder, lightning, and a thick cloud (Exodus 19:16). If the people attempted to approach God, they would be judged by death (Exodus 19:21).*

*Moses was prohibited from seeing God, Who warned him, "You cannot see my face, for no man can see Me and live!"*

*— Paul Enns[8]*

## A. Knowing God

In a study of Heaven the most important aspect in order of importance is the Presence of God and our relationship to Him. We need to focus our mind's attention,

---

[8] *Heaven Revealed*, page 173

our heart's affection, and our will's decision on Him. When we find ourselves longing for or amazed by the reality of Heaven, our longing and our amazement is actually for our relationship to Him. **Knowing God is not to be completely postponed until Heaven.**

We are to practice the presence of God and fellowship with the persons of God now — daily— moment by moment.

Psalm 63:1—

> O God, you are my God, earnestly I seek you; my soul thirsts for you, my body longs for you, in a dry and weary land where there is no water. I have seen you in the sanctuary and beheld your power and your glory. Because your love is better than life, my lips will glorify you.

Randy Alcorn writes,

> Being with God is the heart and soul of Heaven. Every other Heavenly pleasure will derive from and be secondary to His Presence. God's greatest gift to us is, and always will be, Himself.

# B. The "beatific vision"... three Latin words... "a happy-making sight"

**God is transcendent and had been unapproachable in full capacity.[9] However...**

---

[9] "In Christian theology, the beatific vision (Latin: *visio beatifica*) is the ultimate direct self-communication of God to the individual person. A person possessing the beatific vision reaches, as a member of redeemed humanity in the communion of saints, perfect salvation in its entirety, i.e., heaven. The notion of vision stresses the intellectual component of salvation, though it encompasses the whole of human experience of joy, happiness coming from seeing God finally face to face and not imperfectly through faith. (1 Corinthians 13:11–12)." Source = https://en.wikipedia.org/wiki/Beatific_vision, accessed July 28, 2023.

1. **God, who is transcendent, became immanent and fully present when Jesus came to Earth as Immanuel— "God with us."**

   Recall the story.

   Matthew 1:23—

   > *"The virgin will conceive and give birth to a son, and they will call him Immanuel" (which means "God with us").*

   1 John 4:12—

   > *No one has ever seen God; but if we love one another, God lives in us and his love is made complete in us.*

   1 John 3:2—

   > *Dear friends, now we are children of God, and what we will be has not yet been made known. But **we know that when Christ appears, we shall be like him, for we shall see him as he is.***

   Revelation 22:4—

   > *They will see his face, and his name will be on their foreheads.*

2. **When we see Jesus in Heaven, we will see God to an even greater degree than we saw Him before.**

   Recall Jesus' testimony to Philip in John 14:9 and Jesus' promise in Matthew 5:8.

   John 14:9—

   > *Jesus answered: "Don't you know me, Philip, even after I have been among you such a long time? Anyone who has seen me has seen the Father. How can you say, 'Show us the Father'?"*

Jesus came to reveal God to man.

Matthew 5:8—

*Blessed are the pure in heart, for they will see God.*

While it is difficult to comprehend how seeing God face to face will happen, seeing Him will be the primary joy and pleasure of Heaven. Seeing Him will bless us incomprehensibly.

## C. God— the Almighty Creator, Redeemer, Sustainer, Savior, and Lord— is our Father who is in Heaven.

We will live in His presence.

1.  **Not only do we long to be with God, but God has declared His intention for intimate relationship with us.**

    Leviticus 26:11-12—

    *I will put my dwelling place among you, and I will not abhor you. I will walk among you and be your God, and you will be my people.*

    Ezekiel 37:27—

    *My dwelling place will be with them; I will be their God, and they will be my people.*

    2 Corinthians 6:16—

    *What agreement is there between the temple of God and idols?*

*For we are the temple of the living God. As God has said: "I will live with them and walk among them, and I will be their God, and they will be my people."*

2.  **God— and relationship with Him— will be the center around which Heaven revolves.**

    Revelation 21:3—

    *And I heard a loud voice from the throne saying, "Look God's dwelling place is now among the people, and He will dwell with them. They will be His people, and God Himself will be with them and be their God."*

3.  **God's glory won't be isolated to one place in Heaven, however. He will "fill" all of it.**

    Steven J. Lawson states it well.[10]

    *God's glory will fill and permeate the entire New Heaven, not just one centralized place. Thus, wherever we go in Heaven, we will be in the immediate presence of the full glory of God.*

    *Wherever we go, we will enjoy the complete manifestation of God's presence. Throughout all eternity, we will never be separated from direct, unhindered fellowship with God.*

4.  **We will never know all there is to know about God. We will never tire of learning more about Him.**

---

[10] Quoted in Alcorn, *Heaven*, pages 184-185

We will never exhaust the love, joy, peace, fulfillment, and fruitfulness that will be always new and exciting because of Him and how He has provided and will be providing for us.[11]

The most exciting aspect of the universe— past, present, and future eternally — is the presence of God Himself. And we will worship Him and thank Him and treasure Him always.

Notice the inspired writing of King David.

> Psalm 27:4—

>> *One thing I ask of the Lord, this is what I seek: that I may dwell in the house of the Lord all the days of my life, to gaze upon the beauty of the Lord and to seek Him in his temple.*

Jonathan Edwards expressed the grandeur and beauty and joy that God provides.[12]

> *God is the highest good of the reasonable creature, and the enjoyment of him is the only happiness with which our souls can be satisfied. To go to heaven fully to enjoy God is infinitely better than the most pleasant accommodations here.*

# D. Heaven will mean we will be totally with "all" of God— the complete Trinity.

1. **We will be with God the Father— just as Jesus promised in John 14:6.**

---

[11] See point "C" in lesson 11 of this book.

[12] Alcorn, *Heaven*, page 185

John 14:6—

> *"I am the way and the truth and the life. No one comes to the Father except through me."*

We will see Him and we will know Him.

We will marvel and rejoice in His glory.

2. **We will be with Jesus the Son, who also promised He would be there (John 14:2-4).**

John 14:2-4—

> *"My Father's house has many rooms; if that were not so, would I have told you that I am going there to prepare a place for you? And if I go and prepare a place for you, I will come back and take you to be with me that you also may be where I am."*

We will be like Christ. And, we will associate and fellowship with Christ.

3. **We will be with the Holy Spirit.**

The role of the Holy Spirit does not seem to be spelled out in detail regarding Heaven. Perhaps we can surmise a few things, though:

   a. **He will be involved in creating the New Heavens and the New Earth.**

   Genesis 1:2—

   > *Now the earth was formless and empty, darkness was over the surface of the deep, and the Spirit of God was hovering over the waters.*

Isaiah 32:15—

> *… till the Spirit is poured on us from on high, and the desert becomes a fertile field, and the fertile field seems like a forest.*

**b. He will continue to indwell Believers.**

John 16:7—

> *But very truly I tell you, it is for your good that I am going away. Unless I go away, the Advocate will not come to you; but if I go, I will send him to you.*

**c. He will empower us to rule wisely with Christ**

Deuteronomy 34:9—

> *Now Joshua son of Nun was filled with the spirit of wisdom because Moses had laid his hands on him. So the Israelites listened to him and did what the Lord had commanded Moses.*

Judges 3:10—

> *The Spirit of the Lord came on him, so that he became Israel's judge and went to war. The Lord gave Cushan-Rishathaim king of Aram into the hands of Othniel, who overpowered him.*

**d. He may still move us to glorify and worship the Father and the Son.**

John 16:14—

> *He will glorify me because it is from me that he will receive what he will make known to you.*

Revelation 19:1-10—

*After this I heard what sounded like the roar of a great multitude in heaven shouting: "Hallelujah! Salvation and glory and power belong to our God, for true and just are his judgments. He has condemned the great prostitute who corrupted the earth by her adulteries. He has avenged on her the blood of his servants."*

*And again they shouted, "Hallelujah! The smoke from her goes up for ever and ever."*

*The twenty-four elders and the four living creatures fell down and worshiped God, who was seated on the throne.*

*And they cried: "Amen, Hallelujah!"*

*Then a voice came from the throne, saying, "Praise our God, all you his servants, you who fear him, both great and small!"*

*Then I heard what sounded like a great multitude, like the roar of rushing waters and like loud peals of thunder, shouting: "Hallelujah! For our Lord God Almighty reigns. Let us rejoice and be glad and give him glory! For the wedding of the Lamb has come, and his bride has made herself ready. Fine linen, bright and clean, was given her to wear."*

*(Fine linen stands for the righteous acts of God's holy people.)*

*Then the angel said to me, "Write this: Blessed are those who are invited to the wedding supper of the Lamb!"*

*And he added, "These are the true words of God."*

*At this I fell at his feet to worship him.*

*But he said to me, "Don't do that! I am a fellow servant with you and with your brothers and sisters who hold to the testimony of Jesus. Worship God! For it is the Spirit of prophecy who bears testimony to Jesus."*

**e. He will continue as a part of the Trinity.**

Genesis 1:26—

*Then God said, "Let us make mankind in our image, in our likeness, so that they may rule over the fish in the sea and the birds in the sky, over the livestock and all the wild animals, and over all the creatures that move along the ground."*

Hebrews 9:14—

*How much more, then, will the blood of Christ, who through the eternal Spirit offered himself unblemished to God, cleanse our consciences from acts that lead to death, so that we may serve the living God!*

# E. Lessons from Luke 12:37, Matthew 20:28, John 13:8, and Isaiah 25:6.

Notice what these Scriptures say—

Luke 12:37—

*It will be good for those servants whose master finds them watching when he comes. Truly I tell you, he will dress himself to serve, will have them recline at the table and will come and wait on them.*

Matthew 20:28—

*"...just as the Son of Man did not come to be served, but to serve, and to give his life as a ransom for many."*

John 13:8—

*"No," said Peter, "you shall never wash my feet."*

*Jesus answered, "Unless I wash you, you have no part with me."*

Isaiah 25:6—

*On this mountain the Lord Almighty will prepare a feast of rich food for all peoples, a banquet of aged wine the best of meats and the finest of wines.*

# F. Three ways we will worship God.

## 1. We will learn to focus on the Beatific Vision without distraction.

People who love God with all their heart, mind, soul, and strength can never be bored in His presence. The members of the triune godhead exist in eternal and complementary relationship with each other.

To see God and worship God is to participate in the divine delight and joy of the triune communion.

E.J. Forman describes it well.[13]

*What is the essence of Heaven?*

---

[13] E.J. Fortman, quoted by Randy Alcorn, in *Heaven*, page 195

*It is the beatific vision, love, and enjoyment of the triune God. For the three divine persons have an infinitely perfect vision and love and enjoyment of the divine essence and of one another.*

*And in this infinite knowing, loving, and enjoying lies the very life of the triune God, the very essence of their endless and infinite happiness. If the blessed are to be endlessly and supremely happy, then, they must share in the very life of the triune God, in the divine life that makes them endlessly and infinitely happy.*

This indeed is to worship God in spirit and in truth, as we read in John.

John 4:24—

*"God is spirit, and his worshipers must worship in the Spirit and in truth."*

## 2. We will worship God in an all-encompassing way.

It will happen when we bow before Christ on our faces at His feet— as we often envision worship.

However, it will also happen as we serve Him, work for and with Him, fellowship with Him, reign with Him, and even in our eating and drinking while living our eternal lives in Heaven.

See the following verses from Revelation:

Revelation 5:11-14—

*Then I looked and heard the voice of many angels, numbering thousands upon thousands, and ten thousand times ten thousand. They encircled the throne and the living creatures and the elders.*

*In a loud voice they were saying: "Worthy is the Lamb, who was slain, to receive power and wealth and wisdom and strength and honor and glory and praise!"*

*Then I heard every creature in heaven and on earth and under the earth and on the sea, and all that is in them, saying: "To him who sits on the throne and to the Lamb be praise and honor and glory and power, for ever and ever!"*

*The four living creatures said, "Amen," and the elders fell down and worshiped.*

Revelation 7:9-12—

*After this I looked, and there before me was a great multitude that no one could count, from every nation, tribe, people and language, standing before the throne and before the Lamb. They were wearing white robes and were holding palm branches in their hands.*

*And they cried out in a loud voice: "Salvation belongs to our God, who sits on the throne, and to the Lamb."*

*All the angels were standing around the throne and around the elders and the four living creatures.*

*They fell down on their faces before the throne and worshiped God, saying: "Amen! Praise and glory and wisdom and thanks and honor and power and strength be to our God for ever and ever. Amen!"*

Revelation 21:22—

*I did not see a temple in the city, because the Lord God Almighty and the Lamb are its temple.*

3.  **Worship will not and cannot be boring or draining— it will be stirring, captivating, and motivating.**

When a person is consumed with love for another person the time they experience together is joy and delight. The words of the Psalmist express well the yearning that can be filled by only one Person.

Psalm 42:1-2—

*As the deer pants for streams of water, so my soul pants for you, my God. My soul thirsts for God, for the living God. Where can I go and meet with God?*

Worship such as Isaiah experienced will possibly be something like we can expect yet with the curse brought about by sin totally removed. See Isaiah 6 picturing worship in the midst of sinful men.

Worship with the sin and curse gone is demonstrated and will happen in Heaven.

See Revelation 7:13-17 for one glorious pattern and example (a continuation of Revelation 7:9-12, which we referenced on the opposite page.)

Revelation 7:13-17—

*Then one of the elders asked me, "These in white robes—who are they, and where did they come from?"*

*I answered, "Sir, you know."*

*And he said, "These are they who have come out of the great tribulation; they have washed their robes and made them white in the blood of the Lamb."*

*Therefore, they are before the throne of God and serve him day and night in his temple; and he who sits on the throne will shelter them with his presence. Never again will they hunger; never again will they thirst. The sun will not beat down on them, nor any scorching heat.*

*For the Lamb at the center of the throne will be their shepherd; he will lead them to springs of living water. And God will wipe away*

# WORSHIP IN HEAVEN

| Distraction-free | All-encompassing | Captivating |
|---|---|---|
| WE WILL SEE GOD "FULLY," W/ OUT COMMON HINDRANCES | INCLUDES SINGING, SERVING, AND FAR MORE! | WILL BE STIRRING, EMERGING, AND LEAD TO MORE! |

*every tear from their eyes.*

## G. How may/must people prepare for Heaven— our journey there and entry in?

In light of what we have learned, thus far, in part 1 of our study (beginning in lesson 1 when we discussed planning for our journey), consider these three action steps.

**1. Remind yourself that entry into Heaven requires a valid passport.**

Matthew 7:13-23—

*Enter through the narrow gate*. *For wide is the gate and broad is the road that leads to destruction, and many enter through it.*

*But **small is the gate and narrow the road** that leads to life, and only a few find it.*

*Watch out for false prophets. They come to you in sheep's clothing, but inwardly they are ferocious wolves.*

*By their fruit you will recognize them.*

*Do people pick grapes from thorn bushes, or figs from thistles?*

*Likewise, **every good tree bears good fruit**, but a bad tree bears bad fruit. A good tree cannot bear bad fruit, and a bad tree cannot bear good fruit. Every tree that does not bear good fruit is cut down and thrown into the fire.*

*Thus, **by their fruit you will recognize them**.*

*Not everyone who says to me, "Lord, Lord," will enter the kingdom of heaven, but only the one who does the will of my Father who is in heaven.*

*Many will say to me on that day, "Lord, Lord, did we not prophesy in your name and in your name drive out demons and in your name perform many miracles."*

*Then I will tell them plainly, "I never knew you. Away from me, you evildoers!"*

John 3:16-18,36—

*For God so loved the world that he gave his one and only Son, that whoever believes in him shall not perish but have eternal life. **For God did not send his Son into the world to condemn the world, but to save the world through him**.*

*Whoever believes in him is not condemned, but whoever does not believe stands condemned already because they have not believed in the name of God's one and only Son.*

***Whoever believes in the Son has eternal life***, *but whoever rejects the Son will not see life, for God's wrath remains on them.*

Romans 5:1-2—

*Therefore, since we have been justified through faith, we have peace with God through our Lord Jesus Christ, **through whom we have gained access by faith into this grace in which we now stand.** And we boast in the hope of the glory of God.*

Romans 8:1-2—

*Therefore, there is now no condemnation for those who are in Christ Jesus, because **through Christ Jesus the law of the Spirit who gives life has set you free** from the law of sin and death.*

1 John 5:11-13—

*And this is the testimony: **God has given us eternal life, and this life is in his Son.** Whoever has the Son has life; whoever does not have the Son of God does not have life.*

*I write these things to you who believe in the name of the Son of God so that you may know that you have eternal life.*

2. **Live with an eternal perspective. That is, invest time on earth carefully—with an eternal perspective.**

Matthew 6:25-34—

*Therefore I tell you, do not worry about your life, what you will eat or drink; or about your body, what you will wear. Is not life more than food, and the body more than clothes?*

*Look at the birds of the air; they do not sow or reap or store away in barns, and yet your heavenly Father feeds them.*

*Are you not much more valuable than they?*

*Can any one of you by worrying add a single hour to your life?*

*And why do you worry about clothes?*

*See how the flowers of the field grow. They do not labor or spin. Yet I tell you that not even Solomon in all his splendor was dressed like one of these.*

*If that is how God clothes the grass of the field, which is here today and tomorrow is thrown into the fire, will he not much more clothe you—you of little faith?*

*So do not worry, saying, "What shall we eat?" or "What shall we drink?" or "What shall we wear?"*

*For the pagans run after all these things, and your heavenly Father knows that you need them.*

***But seek first his kingdom and his righteousness, and all these things will be given to you as well.***

*Therefore do not worry about tomorrow, for tomorrow will worry about itself. Each day has enough trouble of its own.*

Colossians 3:1-4—

*Since, then, you have been raised with Christ, set your hearts on things above, where Christ is, seated at the right hand of God.*

***Set your minds on things above, not on earthly things.*** *For you died, and your life is now hidden with Christ in God.*

*When Christ, who is your life, appears, then you also will appear with him in glory.*

James 4:13-17—

*Now listen, you who say, "Today or tomorrow we will go to this or that city, spend a year there, carry on business and make money."*

*Why, you do not even know what will happen tomorrow.*

*What is your life?*

*You are a mist that appears for a little while and then vanishes.*

*Instead, you ought to say, "If it is the Lord's will, we will live and do this or that."*

*As it is, you boast in your arrogant schemes. All such boasting is evil. If anyone, then, knows the good they ought to do and doesn't do it, it is sin for them.*

Matthew 25:14-30—

*Again, it will be like a man going on a journey, who called his servants and entrusted his wealth to them. To one he gave five bags of gold, to another two bags, and to another one bag, each according to his ability.*

*Then he went on his journey.*

*The man who had received five bags of gold went at once and put his money to work and gained five bags more. So also, the one with two bags of gold gained two more. But the man who had received one bag went off, dug a hole in the ground and hid his master's money.*

*After a long time the master of those servants returned and settled accounts with them.*

*The man who had received five bags of gold brought the other five. "Master," he said, "you entrusted me with five bags of gold. See, I have gained five more."*

*His master replied, **"Well done, good and faithful servant! You have been faithful with a few things; I will put you in charge of many things. Come and share your master's happiness!"***

*The man with two bags of gold also came.*

*"Master," he said, "you entrusted me with two bags of gold; see, I have gained two more."*

*His master replied, "Well done, good and faithful servant! You have been faithful with a few things; I will put you in charge of many things. Come and share your master's happiness!"*

*Then the man who had received one bag of gold came.*

*"Master," he said, "I knew that you are a hard man, harvesting where you have not sown and gathering where you have not scattered seed. So I was afraid and went out and hid your gold in the ground. See, here is what belongs to you."*

*His master replied, "You wicked, lazy servant! So you knew that I harvest where I have not sown and gather where I have not scattered seed? Well then, you should have put my money on deposit with the bankers, so that when I returned I would have received it back with interest.*

*So take the bag of gold from him and give it to the one who has ten bags. For whoever has will be given more, and they will have an abundance. Whoever does not have, even what they have will be taken from them. And throw that worthless servant outside, into the darkness, where there will be weeping and gnashing of teeth."*

Romans 14:10-12—

*You, then, why do you judge your brother or sister? Or why do you treat them with contempt? **For we will all stand before God's judgment seat.***

*It is written:*

*"As surely as I live," says the Lord, "every knee will bow before me; every tongue will acknowledge God."*

*So then, **each of us will give an account of ourselves to God**.*

2 Corinthians 5:10—

*For we must all appear before the judgment seat of Christ, so that each of us may receive what is due us for the things done while in the body, whether good or bad.*

## THREE WAYS TO PREPARE NOW FOR THE JOURNEY

# 1. PASSPORT
### — INSURE YOU HAVE ONE

# 2. PERSPECTIVE
### — LIVE WITH AN EYE TOWARDS ETERNITY

# 3. PEACE
### — RESOLVE IMPORTANT CONCERNS

3. **Live at peace, by considering your legacy and— as soon as possible— resolving any regrets.**

   Joshua 24:14-15—

*Now fear the Lord and serve him with all faithfulness.* Throw away the gods your ancestors worshiped beyond the Euphrates River and in Egypt, and serve the Lord.

*But if serving the Lord seems undesirable to you, then choose for yourselves this day whom you will serve, whether the gods your ancestors served beyond the Euphrates, or the gods of the Amorites, in whose land you are living. **But as for me and my household, we will serve the Lord.***

Philippians 3:7-14—

*But whatever were gains to me I now consider loss for the sake of Christ. What is more, **I consider everything a loss because of the surpassing worth of knowing Christ Jesus my Lord, for whose sake I have lost all things.** I consider them garbage, that I may gain Christ and be found in him, not having a righteousness of my own that comes from the law, but that which is through faith in Christ—the righteousness that comes from God on the basis of faith.*

*I want to know Christ—yes, to know the power of his resurrection and participation in his sufferings, becoming like him in his death, and so, somehow, attaining to the resurrection from the dead.*

*Not that I have already obtained all this, or have already arrived at my goal, but I press on to take hold of that for which Christ Jesus took hold of me.*

*Brothers and sisters, I do not consider myself yet to have taken hold of it. But one thing I do: **Forgetting what is behind and straining toward what is ahead, I press on toward the goal to win the prize for which God has called me heavenward in Christ Jesus.***

2 Timothy 4:6-8—

*For I am already being poured out like a drink offering, and the time for my departure is near. I have fought the good fight, I have finished the race, I have kept the faith.*

*Now there is in store for me the crown of righteousness, which the Lord, the righteous Judge, will award to me on that day—and not only to me, but also to all who have longed for his appearing.*

### Open My Eyes, That I May See

*Open my eyes, that I may see*
*Glimpses of truth Thou hast for me;*
*Place in my hands the wonderful key*
*That shall unclasp and set me free.*

*Silently now I wait for Thee,*
*Ready my God, Thy will to see,*
*Open my eyes, illumine me,*
*Spirit divine!*

*Open my ears, that I may hear*
*Voices of truth Thou sendest clear;*
*And while the wave notes fall on my ear,*
*Everything false will disappear.*

*Open my mind, that I may read*
*More of Thy love in word and deed;*
*What shall I fear while yet Thou dost lead?*
*Only for light from Thee I plead.*

*Open my mouth, and let me bear,*
*Gladly the warm truth everywhere;*
*Open my heart and let me prepare*
*Love with Thy children thus to share.*

*—Clara H. Scott*

## Face to Face

*Face to face with Christ, my Savior,*
*Face to face—what will it be,*
*When with rapture I behold Him,*
*Jesus Christ who died for me?*

*Face to face I shall behold Him,*
*Far beyond the starry sky;*
*Face to face in all His glory,*
*I shall see Him by and by!*

*Only faintly now I see Him,*
*With the darkened veil between,*
*But a blessed day is coming,*
*When His glory shall be seen.*

*What rejoicing in His presence,*
*When are banished grief and pain;*
*Death is swallowed up in vict'ry,*
*And the dark things shall be plain.*

*—Carrie E. Break*

# Part 2 — Truths to Think About More Often

# 4. Why the Resurrection Means So Much

**Main idea: When Jesus arose from the dead 2,000 years ago, we arose with Him. Furthermore, He became the first fruits of the New Creation, showing what we're destined to become.**

*The major Christian creeds state, "I believe in the resurrection of the body."*

*But I have found in many conversations that Christians tend to spiritualize the resurrection of the dead, effectively denying it.*

*They don't reject it as a doctrine, but they deny its essential meaning: a permanent return to a physical existence in a physical universe.*

*— Randy Alcorn*[14]

---

[14] *Heaven*, page 112

# A. Redemption is physical as well as spiritual—God restores all things.

David Jeremiah, a well-respected long-time Baptist pastor and prolific Christian writer, offers an answer and then offers a couple of questions himself.[15]

> *The Bible consistently teaches the reality of the resurrection, for God created us with eternity in our hearts. We are made for something more than planet earth. We are made for heaven, and we are not going to exist there in a disembodied form.*
>
> *When we die in Christ, our bodies fall asleep and are buried, and our souls go to be with Christ in paradise where we receive temporary bodies until the moment of resurrection.*
>
> *But what then? What will the resurrection be like? What will our resurrection bodies look like and how will they function?*

Matthew, Mark, Luke, and John— the quartet of Gospel writers— offer clear and concise testimony in the closing chapters of their accounts of the Good News of Jesus.

Each wrote, as inspired by the Holy Spirit, about the total fulfillment of the prophecies regarding the death, burial, and resurrection of Jesus Christ.

1.  **Jesus' Resurrection is the model for mankind.**

    Notice the Apostle Paul's account.

    Colossians 1:15-20:

---

[15] David Jeremiah, *The Book of Signs*, page 169

*The Son is the image of the invisible God, the firstborn over all creation. For in him all things were created: things in heaven and on earth, visible and invisible, whether thrones or powers or rulers or authorities; all things have been created through him and for him.*

*He is before all things, and in him all things hold together. And **he is the head of the body, the church; he is the beginning and the firstborn from among the dead**, so that in everything he might have the supremacy.*

*For God was pleased to have all his fullness dwell in him, and through him to reconcile to himself all things, whether things on earth or things in heaven, by making peace through his blood, shed on the cross.*

The "Resurrection Chapter" (1 Corinthians 15) provides a definitive answer to the question referenced in the title of this chapter.

1 Corinthians 15—

*Now, brothers and sisters, I want to remind you of the gospel I preached to you, which you received and on which you have taken your stand. By this gospel you are saved, if you hold firmly to the word I preached to you. Otherwise, you have believed in vain.*

*For what I received I passed on to you as **of first importance: that Christ died for our sins according to the Scriptures, that he was buried, that he was raised on the third day according to the Scriptures**, and that he appeared to Cephas, and then to the Twelve.*

*After that, he appeared to more than five hundred of the brothers and sisters at the same time, most of whom are still living, though some have fallen asleep. Then he appeared to James, then to all the apostles, and last of all he appeared to me also, as to one abnormally born.*

*For I am the least of the apostles and do not even deserve to be called an apostle, because I persecuted the church of God.* **But by the grace of God I am what I am, and his grace to me was not without effect.** *No, I worked harder than all of them—yet not I, but the grace of God that was with me. Whether, then, it is I or they, this is what we preach, and this is what you believed.*

*But if it is preached that Christ has been raised from the dead, how can some of you say that there is no resurrection of the dead?*

*If there is no resurrection of the dead, then not even Christ has been raised. And if Christ has not been raised, our preaching is useless and so is your faith.*

*More than that, we are then found to be false witnesses about God, for we have testified about God that he raised Christ from the dead. But he did not raise him if in fact the dead are not raised. For if the dead are not raised, then Christ has not been raised either. And if Christ has not been raised, your faith is futile; you are still in your sins. Then those also who have fallen asleep in Christ are lost. If only for this life we have hope in Christ, we are of all people most to be pitied.*

**But Christ has indeed been raised from the dead, the firstfruits of those who have fallen asleep. For since death came through a man, the resurrection of the dead comes also through a man. For as in Adam all die, so in Christ all will be made alive.** *But each in turn: Christ, the firstfruits; then, when he comes, those who belong to him. Then the end will come, when he hands over the kingdom to God the Father after he has destroyed all dominion, authority and power. For he must reign until he has put all his enemies under his feet.*

*The last enemy to be destroyed is death. For he has put everything under his feet.*

Now when it says that "everything" has been put under him, it is clear that this does not include God himself, who put everything under Christ. When he has done this, then the Son himself will be made subject to him who put everything under him, so that God may be all in all.

Now if there is no resurrection, what will those do who are baptized for the dead? If the dead are not raised at all, why are people baptized for them?

And as for us, why do we endanger ourselves every hour? I face death every day—yes, just as surely as I boast about you in Christ Jesus our Lord. If I fought wild beasts in Ephesus with no more than human hopes, what have I gained?

If the dead are not raised, "Let us eat and drink, for tomorrow we die."

Do not be misled: "Bad company corrupts good character."

Come back to your senses as you ought, and stop sinning; for there are some who are ignorant of God—I say this to your shame.

But someone will ask, "How are the dead raised? With what kind of body will they come?"

How foolish! What you sow does not come to life unless it dies.

When you sow, you do not plant the body that will be, but just a seed, perhaps of wheat or of something else.

But God gives it a body as he has determined, and to each kind of seed he gives its own body. Not all flesh is the same: People have one kind of flesh, animals have another, birds another and fish another. There are also heavenly bodies and there are earthly bodies; but the splendor of the heavenly bodies is one kind, and the splendor of the earthly bodies is another. The sun has one kind of *splendor, the moon another and the stars another; and star differs from star in splendor.*

***So will it be with the resurrection of the dead. The body that is sown is perishable, it is raised imperishable***; *it is sown in dishonor, it is raised in glory; it is sown in weakness, it is raised in power; it is sown a natural body, it is raised a spiritual body.*

*If there is a natural body, there is also a spiritual body.*

*So it is written: "The first man Adam became a living being"; the last Adam, a life-giving spirit.*

*The spiritual did not come first, but the natural, and after that the spiritual. The first man was of the dust of the earth; the second man is of heaven. As was the earthly man, so are those who are of the earth; and as is the heavenly man, so also are those who are of heaven. And just as we have borne the image of the earthly man, so shall we bear the image of the heavenly man.*

*I declare to you, brothers and sisters, that flesh and blood cannot inherit the kingdom of God, nor does the perishable inherit the imperishable.*

*Listen, I tell you a mystery: We will not all sleep, but **we will all be changed— in a flash, in the twinkling of an eye, at the last trumpet**. For the trumpet will sound, the dead will be raised imperishable, and we will be changed. **For the perishable must clothe itself with the imperishable, and the mortal with immortality**. When the perishable has been clothed with the imperishable, and the mortal with immortality, then the saying that is written will come true: **"Death has been swallowed up in victory."***

*Where, O death, is your victory?*

*Where, O death, is your sting?*

*The sting of death is sin, and the power of sin is the law. But thanks be to God! He gives us the victory through our Lord Jesus Christ.*

*Therefore, my dear brothers and sisters, stand firm. Let nothing move you. Always give yourselves fully to the work of the Lord, because you know that your labor in the Lord is not in vain.*

**We know what our present bodies are like. We also have a Scriptural model of what our Resurrection body will be like.** The Gospel of Luke offers insight through the words of our Lord Jesus after His Resurrection.

Luke 24:39—

*"Look at my hands and my feet. **It is I myself!** Touch me and see; a ghost does not have flesh and bones, as you see I have."*

Following the Resurrection, Jesus walked the earth 40 days giving prior evidence and a model example as to how we will live as resurrected human beings on the New Heaven and New Earth.

Jesus walked and talked with two disciples on the Emmaus Road. They were unaware they were walking and talking with the Lord Jesus.

Mary called Him "Sir," thinking He was the gardener until He spoke her name as only He could.

John 20:15-16—

*He asked her, "Woman, why are you crying? Who is it you are looking for?"*

*Thinking he was the gardener, she said, "Sir, if you have carried him away, tell me where you have put him, and I will get him."*

*Jesus said to her, "Mary."*

*She turned toward him and cried out in Aramaic, "Rabboni!" (which means "Teacher").*

Following His Resurrection John 21 describes that Jesus lived what was essentially "normal life." Jesus is seen standing on the shore, starting a fire, cooking, and interacting with those persons who were present.

> John 21:9-12—
>
> *When they landed, they saw a fire of burning coals there with fish on it, and some bread.*
>
> *Jesus said to them, "Bring some of the fish you have just caught."*
>
> *So Simon Peter climbed back into the boat and dragged the net ashore. It was full of large fish, 153, but even with so many the net was not torn.*
>
> *Jesus said to them, "Come and have breakfast."*
>
> *None of the disciples dared ask him, "Who are you?"*
>
> ***They knew it was the Lord.***

Jesus could be touched, clung to, able to cook, and eat food. He could materialize.

## 2. Jesus' Resurrection is the gateway for all of Creation.

Paul offers statements about even Creation itself waiting patiently for renewal and restoration that is dependent on the Resurrection.

> Romans 8:18-23—
>
> *I consider that our present sufferings are not worth comparing with the glory that will be revealed in us.*
>
> *For the creation waits in eager expectation for the children of God to be revealed. For the creation was subjected to frustration, not by its own choice, but by the will of the one who subjected it, **in hope that***

*the creation itself will be liberated from its bondage to decay and brought into the freedom and glory of the children of God.*

*We know that the whole creation has been groaning as in the pains of childbirth right up to the present time.*

*Not only so, but we ourselves, who have the first fruits of the Spirit, groan inwardly as **we wait eagerly for our adoption to sonship, the redemption of our bodies...***

We read much the same at the end of the New Testament.

Revelation 21:1-3—

*Then I saw "a new heaven and a new earth," for the first heaven and the first earth had passed away, and there was no longer any sea.*

*I saw the Holy City, the new Jerusalem, coming down out of heaven from God, prepared as a bride beautifully dressed for her husband.*

*And I heard a loud voice from the throne saying, "Look! God's dwelling place is now among the people, and he will dwell with them. They will be his people, and God himself will be with them and be their God.*

3. **Jesus' Resurrection will be our reality, too!**

Jesus was raised. We will be raised!

1 Thessalonians 4:14—

*For we believe that Jesus died and rose again, and so we believe that God will bring with Jesus those who have fallen asleep in him.*

The "beloved disciple," John, offered yet another aspect of the importance of the Resurrection.

1 John 3:1-3—

> *See what great love the Father has lavished on us, that we should be called children of God! And that is what we are! The reason the world does not know us is that it did not know him.*
>
> *Dear friends, now we are children of God, and what we will be has not yet been made known.* **But we know that when Christ appears, we shall be like him, for we shall see him as he is.**
>
> *All who have this hope in him purify themselves, just as he is pure.*

That means that Christ's resurrected life is a model for our lives when resurrected at that glorious moment in our life journeys.

Philippians 3:20-21—

> *But our citizenship is in heaven. And we eagerly await a Savior from there, the Lord Jesus Christ, who, by the power that enables him to bring everything under his control,* **will transform our lowly bodies so that they will be like his glorious body.**

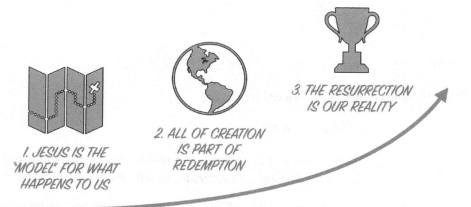

1. JESUS IS THE 'MODEL' FOR WHAT HAPPENS TO US

2. ALL OF CREATION IS PART OF REDEMPTION

3. THE RESURRECTION IS OUR REALITY

## THREE REASONS THE RESURRECTION MATTERS

# B. What will our resurrected bodies be like?

11 observations about our resurrected body.

### 1. Jesus' resurrected life is the model for our new bodies.

Notice that Jesus shows us what we will be like— who we are designed to be.

Colossians 1:15—

*The Son is the image of the invisible God, **the firstborn over all***
***creation.***

1 Corinthians 15:20-23—

*But Christ has indeed been raised from the dead, the firstfruits of*
*those who have fallen asleep. For since death came through a man,*
***the resurrection of the dead comes also through a man.***

*For as in Adam all die, so in Christ all will be made alive. But each in*
*turn: Christ, the firstfruits; then, when he comes, those who belong to*
*him.*

When speaking of our citizenship in Heaven, Paul highlighted the transformation of our bodies.

Philippians 3:20-21—

*But our citizenship is in heaven. And we eagerly await a Savior from*
*there, the Lord Jesus Christ, who, by the power that enables him to*
*bring everything under his control, **will transform our lowly bodies***
***so that they will be like his glorious body.***

Before writing this, Paul had encountered the glorified Jesus on the Road to Damascus.

Acts 22:6-11—

> About noon as I came near Damascus, suddenly a bright light from heaven flashed around me. I fell to the ground and heard a voice say to me, "Saul! Saul! Why do you persecute me?"
>
> "Who are you, Lord?" I asked.
>
> **"I am Jesus of Nazareth, whom you are persecuting,"** he replied.
>
> My companions saw the light, but they did not understand the voice of him who was speaking to me.
>
> "'What shall I do, Lord?" I asked.
>
> "Get up," the Lord said, "'and go into Damascus. There you will be told all that you have been assigned to do."
>
> My companions led me by the hand into Damascus, because **the brilliance of the light had blinded me.**

Paul (Saul) was present even earlier than this when Stephen saw a glimpse of the glorified Jesus.

Acts 7:55-56—

> But Stephen, full of the Holy Spirit, looked up to heaven and saw the glory of God, and Jesus standing at the right hand of God.
>
> "Look," he said, "I see heaven open and the Son of Man standing at the right hand of God."

Before these encounters, **the Transfiguration also provided a precursor to the glorified state of being..**

Matthew 17:2—

> There he was transfigured before them. His face shone like the sun, and his clothes became as white as the light.

And, John saw Jesus in **His glorified expression** when he received the Revelation account.

Revelation 1:12-18—

> *I turned around to see the voice that was speaking to me.*
>
> *And when I turned I saw seven golden lamp stands, and among the lamp stands was someone like a son of man, dressed in a robe reaching down to his feet and with a golden sash around his chest.*
>
> *The hair on his head was white like wool, as white as snow, and his eyes were like blazing fire.*
>
> *His feet were like bronze glowing in a furnace, and his voice was like the sound of rushing waters.*
>
> *In his right hand he held seven stars, and coming out of his mouth was a sharp, double-edged sword. His face was like the sun shining in all its brilliance.*
>
> *When I saw him, I fell at his feet as though dead.*
>
> *Then he placed his right hand on me and said: "Do not be afraid. I am the First and the Last. I am the Living One; I was dead, and now look, I am alive for ever and ever! And I hold the keys of death and Hades."*

Some aspects of Jesus' Resurrection Body may be different and unique. He is the God/Man—totally human (perfectly), totally Divine. Yet He certainly shows us what's coming.

Speaking of this, the renowned preacher Charles Spurgeon said—

> *We have been redeemed by the price paid, but not yet by the power applied.*

2.  **We will have intermediate, temporary bodies in the "present Heaven."**

    We will be recognizable persons. Moses and Elijah were recognized at the Transfiguration. Peter wanted to build tents.

    > Matthew 17:3—

    > > *Just then there appeared before them Moses and Elijah, talking with Jesus.*

    > 2 Corinthians 5:6-8—

    > > *Therefore we are always confident and know that as long as we are at home in the body we are away from the Lord. For we live by faith, not by sight. We are confident, I say, and would prefer to be away from the body and at home with the Lord.*

    Randy Alcorn suggests of this—

    *God may grant us some physical form that will allow us to function as humans between the time of our death awaiting the time of resurrection.*[16]

3.  **There will be critical continuity between our bodies now and then.**

    > Luke 24:42-43—

    > > *They gave him a piece of broiled fish, and he took it and ate it in their presence.*

    There is an intimate connection between our bodies and our souls. Man is soul-mind-body-emotion-will. We must have both spirit and body to be

---

[16] Alcorn, *Heaven*, page 57

completely human. There is to be a continuity between what we have now and our resurrection bodies.

We will be the same persons then as we are now in terms of identity and continuity even though we will be "changed," so that we may be fully redeemed and perfected to God to glorify the greatness of our Creator and Redeemer.

4. **Our final bodies will be like Christ's.**

We will be the recipients of bodies similar in kind to Jesus' Resurrection body.

We will bear two images: the image of the earthly man and the image of the heavenly man.

1 John 3:2—

> *Dear friends, now we are children of God, and what we will be has not yet been made known. But we know that when Christ appears,* ***we shall be like him, for we shall see him as he is.***

1 Corinthians 15:49—

> *And just as we have borne the image of the earthly man,* ***so shall we bear the image of the heavenly man.***

Romans 8:29-30—

> ***For those God foreknew he also predestined to be conformed to the image of his Son,*** *that he might be the firstborn among many brothers and sisters. And those he predestined, he also called; those he called, he also justified; those he justified, he also glorified.*

In our final bodies, I will be me and you will be you. Our earthly body will be transformed into a body that looks like us. God uniquely created each of us.

5. **We will have a real physical / spiritual body.**

   1 Corinthians 15:3-8—

   > For what I received I passed on to you as of first importance: that Christ died for our sins according to the Scriptures, that he was buried, that he was raised on the third day according to the Scriptures, and that he appeared to Cephas, and then to the Twelve.
   >
   > After that, he appeared to more than five hundred of the brothers and sisters at the same time, most of whom are still living, though some have fallen asleep.
   >
   > Then he appeared to James, then to all the apostles, and last of all he appeared to me also, as to one abnormally born.

6. **We will have a recognizable body and a familiar voice.**

   Mary was in the garden near the tomb, grieving over the death of Jesus.

   He called to her, "Mary."

   That is when she recognized Him in His resurrected body. It was the same tone in His voice she had known and treasured. Mary possibly had not recognized Jesus because her eyes were blurred by tears and sorrow.

   John 20:11-16—

   > Now Mary stood outside the tomb crying. As she wept, she bent over to look into the tomb and saw two angels in white, seated where Jesus' body had been, one at the head and the other at the foot.
   >
   > They asked her, "Woman, why are you crying?"

*"They have taken my Lord away," she said, "and I don't know where they have put him."*

*At this, she turned around and saw Jesus standing there, but she did not realize that it was Jesus.*

*He asked her, "Woman, why are you crying? Who is it you are looking for?"*

*Thinking he was the gardener, she said, "Sir, if you have carried him away, tell me where you have put him, and I will get him."*

*Jesus said to her, "Mary."*

*She turned toward him and cried out in Aramaic, "Rabboni!" (which means "Teacher").*

People I know have voices I recognize.

It is so good to hear a voice that has a calming effect. A voice that lends an encouraging sound to the ear. A voice that gives one a sense of closeness, comfort, and challenge.

We will be both recognizable in appearance and a familiar sound, our voice. I believe we will recognize voices just as Mary recognized the familiar voice of her Lord Jesus.

Recognition of our familiar voices does not necessarily mean that we will continue to miss notes when we sing.

Will a monotone still be a monotone? Will all of us be Carusos?

One thing is sure, there will be a beauty of the heavenly singing and choirs.

1 Thessalonians 4:16-17—

*For the Lord himself will come down from heaven, with a loud command, with the voice of the archangel and with the trumpet call of God, and the dead in Christ will rise first. After that, we who are still alive and are left will be caught up together with them…*

## 7. We will have an imperishable body.

We will have a body that will evidently preserved from the deteriorating aspects we now have in these perishable bodies. No more headaches, stomach aches, diabetes, cancer, heart ailments…

We will have perfect bodies resistant to harm, disease, and death. There will be no more sin, decay, or destructibility.

The physical problems we face today will be gone!

> 1 Corinthians 15:43-44—
>
> *So will it be with the resurrection of the dead.* **The body that is sown is perishable, it is raised imperishable; it is sown in dishonor, it is raised in glory**; *it is sown in weakness, it is raised in power; it is sown a natural body, it is raised a spiritual body.*
>
> *If there is a natural body, there is also a spiritual body.*

## 8. We will have a glorified body.

The "glorified body" is still a mystery, but a guaranteed reality to be experienced. There are beautiful people on earth. In Heaven we will see beauty in essence and beyond our fleshly limitations.

Commentators suggest that the "resurrected body" will exhibit that resplendent brightness fashioned like the glorious body so many of our spiritual ancestors saw when they encountered Jesus.

> 1 Corinthians 15:53-54—

*For the perishable must clothe itself with the imperishable, and the mortal with immortality. When the perishable has been clothed with the imperishable, and the mortal with immortality, then the saying that is written will come true: "Death has been swallowed up in victory."*

The chorus of the old song made popular by Burl Ives comes to mind.[17]

*Brighten the corner where you are*
*Brighten the corner where you are*
*Someone far from harbor you may guide across the bar*
*Brighten the corner where you are*

9. **We will have a strong body.**

Having a strong body does not mean we will look like Arnold Schwarzenegger or any body-builder. Pure strength was revealed in Jesus and will be revealed in Jesus.

And we will be like Him.

There will be no physical, emotional, or mental pain or weakness.

Robert Gromache says, "There is no indication that we will need sleep or food."[18]

However, some people like to sleep and many of us like to eat. Maybe we will do a mixture of both (we do see feasts in Heaven[19])— not of necessity but by choice.

Revelation 21:4—

---

[17] *Brighten Where You Are*

[18] Quoted by Paul Enns, *Heaven Revealed*, p. 80

[19] Revelation 19:6-9, Isaiah 25:6-9

*He will wipe every tear from their eyes. There will be no more death or mourning... the old order of things has passed away.*

Revelation 22:1-2—

*Then the angel showed me the river of the water of life, as clear as crystal, flowing from the throne of God and of the Lamb down the middle of the great street of the city. On each side of the river stood the tree of life, bearing twelve crops of fruit, yielding its fruit every month. **And the leaves of the tree are for the healing of the nations.***

## 10. We will have a body without limitations.

One of the first times Jesus appeared to His disciples post-Resurrection, He moved into a locked room. Notice—

John 20:19—

*On the evening of that first day of the week, when the disciples were together, **with the doors locked for fear of the Jewish leaders, Jesus came and stood among them** and said, "Peace be with you!"*

This wasn't an isolated incident.

John 20:26—

***A week later** his disciples were in the house again, and Thomas was with them. **Though the doors were locked**, Jesus came and stood among them and said, "Peace be with you!"*

Apparently, He not only "appeared" suddenly, He also vanished suddenly as well. Remember the experience of the two disciples He met on the Road to Emmaus.

Luke 24:31—

> Then their eyes were opened and they recognized him, **and he disappeared from their sight.**

Notice, these two traveled back to Jerusalem to tell the disciples, at which point Jesus re-appeared.

Luke 24:36—

> **While they were still talking about this, Jesus himself stood among them** and said to them, "Peace be with you."

Jesus could evidently appear and disappear as needed. He had a physical body of flesh and bones but could pass through doors unhindered by locks.

Though we really don't know what our capacity will be in the future, it seems we will not be hindered in some ways God has "more" in His perfect, abiding plan for us.

Remember, as we've seen throughout our study, something different— and better— is coming.

Philippians 3:20-21—

> But our citizenship is in heaven. And we eagerly await a Savior from there, the Lord Jesus Christ, who, by the power that enables him to bring everything under his control, **will transform our lowly bodies so that they will be like his glorious body.**

The limitations that will be removed will be at God's discretion. Some things we consider limits now may not be limits then. The perfections (completions, fulfillment of our eternal purpose) we receive will be according to God's plan.

Randy Alcorn reminds us that "we are not explicitly told what we will be able to do" when that time comes.[20]

---

[20] See his book *Heaven*, page 118.

We will be able to stretch and be expanded, because of our perfected (completed) human bodies. Some changes may seem to be supernatural compared to what we now know. Yet, recall a truth we've stated and affirmed throughout this resource: **we are *already* supernatural.**

Twice born + gifted capacities = SUPERNATURAL.

However, we are not yet free from the temptations and inclinations of present earth. In the future, that will change— indeed, we will be changed.

## 11. We will have an eternal body.

Eternal bodies are beyond our ability to comprehend currently. We would need to be endowed with a fuller ability to understand and perception that exceeds our current capacities and boundaries. And that is what is coming.

> Revelation 22:5—

> *There will be no more night. They will not need the light of a lamp or the light of the sun, for the Lord God will give them light. And they will reign for ever and ever.*

Note what Joni Erickson Tada says about this final point.[21]

> *Somewhere in my broken, paralyzed body is the seed of what I shall become. The paralysis makes what I am to become all the more grand when you contrast atrophied, useless legs against splendorous resurrected legs. I'm convinced that if there are mirrors in heaven (and why not?), the image I'll see will be unmistakably Joni, although a much better, brighter Joni.*

Robert Jeffress reminds us that all men are created for eternity.[22]

---

[21] Quoted by Randy Alcorn in *50 Days of Heaven*, page 97

[22] Jeffress, *A Place Called Heaven*, page 152.

*Just as Christians will receive physical bodies in which they can enjoy the eternal benefits of the New Heaven and New Earth, unbelievers will be resurrected and receive physical bodies in which to endure the eternal torment of the lake of fire.*

## Resurrection Power

| OUR EARTHLY BODY | OUR HEAVENLY BODY |
| --- | --- |
| Sown in a perishable body | Raised imperishable, incorruptible |
| Sown in dishonor | Raised in glory |
| Sown in weakness | Raised in power |
| Sown natural | Raised spiritual, supernatural |

**Christ the Lord is Risen Today**

*Christ the Lord is ris'n today, Alleluia!*
*Sons of men and angels say, Alleluia!*
*Raise your joys and triumphs high, Alleluia!*
*Sing, ye heav'ns, and earth, reply, Alleluia!*

*Lives again our glorious King, Alleluia!*
*Where, O death, is now thy sting? Alleluia!*

*Once He died our souls to save, Alleluia!*
*Where thy victory, O grave? Alleluia!*

*Love's redeeming work is done, Alleluia!*
*Fought the fight, the battle won, Alleluia!*
*Death in vain forbids His rise, Alleluia!*
*Christ hath opened paradise, Alleluia!*

*Soar we now where Christ hath led, Alleluia!*
*Foll'wing our exalted Head, Alleluia!*
*Made like Him, like Him we rise, Alleluia!*
*Ours the cross, the grave, the skies, Alleluia!*

*Hail the Lord of earth and heaven, Alleluia!*
*Praise to Thee by both be given, Alleluia!*
*Thee we greet triumphant now, Alleluia!*
*Hail the Resurrection, thou, Alleluia!*

*King of glory, Soul of bliss, Alleluia!*
*Everlasting life is this, Alleluia!*
*Thee to know, Thy pow'r to prove, Alleluia!*
*Thus to sing, and thus to love, Alleluia!*

*—Charles Wesley*

### Since I Have Been Redeemed

*I have a song I love to sing,*
*Since I have been redeemed,*
*Of my Redeemer, Savior king,*
*Since I have been redeemed.*

*Since I have been redeemed,*
*Since I have been redeemed,*
*I will glory in His name;*
*Since I have been redeemed,*
*I will glory in the Savior's name.*

*I have a Christ who satisfies*
*Since I have been redeemed;*
*To do His will my highest prize,*
*Since I have been redeemed.*

*I have a witness bright and clear,*
*Since I have been redeemed,*
*Dispelling every doubt and fear,*
*Since I have been redeemed.*

*I have a home prepared for me,*
*Since I have been redeemed,*
*Where I shall dwell eternally,*
*Since I have been redeemed.*

*I have a joy I can't express,*
*Since I have been redeemed,*
*All through His blood and righteousness,*
*Since I have been redeemed.*

*—Edwin O. Excell*

# 4. Why the Resurrection Means So Much

# 5. Our Role in Ruling with Christ

**Main idea: From the beginning of time, we discover that we were created for relationship and rulership. Although the Fall postponed our potential, it didn't eliminate— or change— it.**

*Earth exists for the very same reason that mankind and everything else exists: to glorify God. God is glorified when we take our rightful, intended place in His creation and exercise the dominion that He bestowed upon us. God appointed human beings to rule the earth (see Genesis 1:26-28).*

*God's intention for humans was that we would occupy the whole earth and reign over it. This dominion would produce God-exalting societies in which we would exercise creativity, imagination, intellect, and skills befitting beings created in God's image, thereby manifesting His attributes.*

*— Randy Alcorn*[23]

[23] *Heaven*, page 125

# A. Why God created mankind and the earth and the universe— back to the beginning

### 1. We were designed to rule / reign.

It seems clear that God's original intention for mankind was for us to occupy the whole Earth and reign over the Earth— and whatever else God made to live on Earth.

Genesis 1:26-28—

> Then God said, "Let us make mankind in our image, in our likeness, **so that they may rule** over the fish in the sea and the birds in the sky, over the livestock and all the wild animals, and over all the creatures that move along the ground."
>
> So God created mankind in his own image— in the image of God he created them; male and female he created them.
>
> God blessed them and said to them, "Be fruitful and increase in number; fill the earth and subdue it. **Rule over the fish in the sea and the birds in the sky and over every living creature that moves on the ground."**

God gave specific job descriptions in Genesis— to rule and reign— to cultivate and care as co-regents over creation in essence as king and queen of Earth.

Robert Jeffress writes—

> Because of a conscious decision to sinfully disobey God's simple limiting instruction (which was for their own good) they were forced to abdicate their reign to a degree.[24]

---

[24] Jeffress, *A Place Called Heaven*, page 110

## 2. We were designed for relationship.

God made man for relationship and expanded that to include man and woman also in relationship.

Jonathan Edwards wrote,

> *He chose to create the Heavens and the Earth so that His glory could come pouring out from Himself in abundance. He brought a physical reality into existence in order that it might experience His glory and be filled with it and reflect it— every second, every part and every moment of creation. He made human beings in His own image to reflect His glory, and He placed them in a perfect environment which also reflected it.*[25]

Some people may object to this line of reasoning (as I did at one time): "Wait a minute! How dare we imagine such for ourselves?"

As Randy Alcorn says, "Claiming these things would be blasphemous if it was our idea. Not so, though, since it is God's plan!"[26]

One day when Christ returns, He will establish a thousand year reign on earth— the Millennium. That period will extend beyond our timeline and into the eternality of the New Heaven and New Earth.

Daniel 7:18—

> *But the holy people of the Most High will receive the kingdom and will possess it forever—yes, for ever and ever.*

Daniel 7:27—

> *Then the sovereignty, power and greatness of all the kingdoms under heaven will be handed over to the holy people of the Most*

---

[25] Quoted by Randy Alcorn, *Heaven*, page 226

[26] *Alcorn, Heaven*, page 225

*High. His kingdom will be an everlasting kingdom, and all rulers will worship and obey him.*

This is, as Jonathan Edwards termed it, "The End for which God created the world."

# B. The Fall— and the fix.

**It is important that we base our identity on God's Creation-intention— and His Redemption— not the Fall.**

God is glorified when His created beings do what He designed them to do. God's intention for mankind was that man would occupy the earth that He made perfectly and reign as obedient stewards over it.

Remember the key words in Genesis 1:26-28: "Let them have dominion."

The world as it was in the beginning was good. God said so, repeatedly.[27]

The world as it is now is fallen. We are now under the curse that was the result of disobedience (sin). The condition is not permanent. There is a remedy God provided: the redemptive work of Jesus.

1. **The roles of Adam and Eve = ruling the earth for the glory of God.**

   See Genesis 1:26-28 (beginning of chapter), as well as the following.

   1 Peter 1:3-5—

---

[27] God declared it was "good" in Genesis 1:4, 10, 12, 18, 21, 25. On the sixth day, after creating the man and the woman, He said it was "*very* good" (see 1:31).

*Praise be to the God and Father of our Lord Jesus Christ!* **In his great mercy he has given us new birth into a living hope through the resurrection of Jesus Christ** *from the dead, and into an inheritance that can never perish, spoil or fade.*

*This inheritance is kept in heaven for you, who through faith are shielded by God's power until the coming of the* **salvation that is ready to be revealed in the last time.**

2. **Redemption— and Heaven— reveal a restoration of mankind's position, role, and responsibility.**

   Genesis 3:14-20—

   *So the Lord God said to the serpent, "Because you have done this, cursed are you above all livestock and all wild animals! You will crawl on your belly and you will eat dust all the days of your life. And I will put enmity between you and the woman, and between your offspring and hers; he will crush your head, and you will strike his heel."*

   *To the woman he said, "I will make your pains in childbearing very severe; with painful labor you will give birth to children. Your desire will be for your husband, and he will rule over you."*

   *To Adam he said, "Because you listened to your wife and ate fruit from the tree about which I commanded you, 'You must not eat from it,' cursed is the ground because of you; through painful toil you will eat food from it all the days of your life. It will produce thorns and thistles for you, and you will eat the plants of the field. By the sweat of your brow you will eat your food until you return to the ground, since from it you were taken; for dust you are and to dust you will return."*

   *Adam named his wife Eve, because she would become the mother of all the living.*

John 1:9-13—

> *The true light that gives light to everyone was coming into the world.*
> *He was in the world, and though the world was made through him,*
> *the world did not recognize him. He came to that which was his own,*
> *but his own did not receive him.*
>
> *Yet to all who did receive him, to those who believed in his name, he*
> *gave the right to become children of God— children born not of*
> *natural descent, nor of human decision or a husband's will, but born*
> *of God.*

Luke 22:29-30—

> *And I confer on you a kingdom, just as my Father conferred one on*
> *me, so that you may eat and drink at my table in my kingdom and **sit***
> ***on thrones, judging the twelve tribes of Israel.***

Matthew 25:23—

> *His master replied, "Well done, good and faithful servant! You have*
> *been faithful with a few things; **I will put you in charge of many***
> ***things.** Come and share your master's happiness!"*

# C. The outcome: a fully-restored relationship and a reinstatement of our role.

When we read Revelation we see a realignment to God reigning uncontested with mankind serving Him.

Think of this.

When you think of Jesus what character traits come to mind?

Certainly not boisterous, pushy or proud.

What about the indicators of the Fruit of the Spirit recorded in Galatians 5:22-23 and the admonition expressed by Peter in 2 Peter 1:3-11.

Galatians 5:22-23—

> But the fruit of the Spirit is **love, joy, peace, forbearance, kindness, goodness, faithfulness, gentleness and self-control.** Against such things there is no law.

2 Peter 1:3-11—

> His divine power has given us everything we need for a godly life through our knowledge of him who called us by his own glory and goodness.
>
> Through these he has given us his very great and precious promises, so that through them you may participate in the divine nature, having escaped the corruption in the world caused by evil desires.
>
> For this very reason, make every effort to **add to your faith goodness; and to goodness, knowledge; and to knowledge, self-control; and to self-control, perseverance; and to perseverance, godliness; and to godliness, mutual affection; and to mutual affection, love.**
>
> For if you possess these qualities in increasing measure, they will keep you from being ineffective and unproductive in your knowledge of our Lord Jesus Christ.
>
> But whoever does not have them is nearsighted and blind, forgetting that they have been cleansed from their past sins.
>
> Therefore, my brothers and sisters, make every effort to confirm your calling and election. For if you do these things, you will never stumble, and you will receive a rich welcome into the eternal kingdom of our Lord and Savior Jesus Christ.

God resides in— and embodies— glory. Furthermore, the glory in which we reside will be provided by Him and will glorify Him.

1.   **The glory in which God resides, God also provides.**

Psalm 19:1-2–

> **The heavens declare the glory of God;** *the skies proclaim the work of his hands. Day after day they pour forth speech; night after night they reveal knowledge.*

Psalm 72:18-19–

> *Praise be to the Lord God, the God of Israel, who alone does marvelous deeds. Praise be to his glorious name forever;* **may the whole earth be filled with his glory.** *Amen and Amen.*

Psalm 102:15-16—

> *The nations will fear the name of the Lord, all the kings of the earth will revere your glory.* **For the Lord will rebuild Zion and appear in his glory.**

Isaiah11:9-10—

> *They will neither harm nor destroy on all my holy mountain, for* **the earth will be filled with the knowledge of the Lord as the waters cover the sea.** *In that day the Root of Jesse will stand as a banner for the peoples; the nations will rally to him, and his resting place will be glorious.*

Isaiah 40:5—

> **And the glory of the Lord will be revealed,** *and all people will see it together. For the mouth of the Lord has spoken.*

Isaiah 66:19-20—

*"I will set a sign among them, and I will send some of those who survive to the nations—to Tarshish, to the Libyans and Lydians (famous as archers), to Tubal and Greece, and to the distant islands that have not heard of my fame or seen my glory.* **They will proclaim my glory among the nations.**

*"And they will bring all your people, from all the nations, to my holy mountain in Jerusalem as an offering to the Lord—on horses, in chariots and wagons, and on mules and camels," says the Lord. "They will bring them, as the Israelites bring their grain offerings, to the temple of the Lord in ceremonially clean vessels…"*

Haggai 2:6-7—

*This is what the Lord Almighty says: "In a little while I will once more shake the heavens and the earth, the sea and the dry land. I will shake all nations, and what is desired by all nations will come, and* **I will fill this house with glory**," *says the Lord Almighty.*

Romans 8:16-17—

*The Spirit himself testifies with our spirit that we are God's children. Now if we are children, then we are heirs—heirs of God and co-heirs with Christ, if indeed we share in his sufferings in order that* **we may also share in his glory**.

## 2. The position and the promises revealed in Revelation.

Those who rule and reign in Heaven will be those who have the desire and the capacity to do as God calls and equips.

Many faithful Christians do not feel or desire that they should be in charge. Unless God so fits them, they will not be forced into such roles. Some of us feel quite fulfilled— and are fruitful— serving behind the scenes… in the background… with a sense of joyful purpose.

Others enjoy leading.

Whatever the case, however God uniquely created each of us, Robert Jeffress reminds us, "What you do on earth echoes in the halls of Heaven."[28]

Recall the parable of the minas.

Luke 19:11-27—

> *While they were listening to this, he went on to tell them a parable, because he was near Jerusalem and the people thought that the kingdom of God was going to appear at once. He said:*
>
> *A man of noble birth went to a distant country to have himself appointed king and then to return.*
>
> *So he called ten of his servants and gave them ten minas. '*
>
> *"Put this money to work," he said, "until I come back."*
>
> *But his subjects hated him and sent a delegation after him to say, "We don't want this man to be our king."*
>
> *He was made king, however, and returned home.*
>
> *Then he sent for the servants to whom he had given the money, in order to find out what they had gained with it.*
>
> *The first one came and said, "Sir, your mina has earned ten more."*
>
> *"'Well done, my good servant!" his master replied. "Because you have been trustworthy in a very small matter, take charge of ten cities."*
>
> *The second came and said, "Sir, your mina has earned five more."*
>
> *His master answered, "You take charge of five cities."*

---

[28] Jeffress, *A Place Called Heaven*, page 112

*Then another servant came and said, "Sir, here is your mina; I have kept it laid away in a piece of cloth. I was afraid of you, because you are a hard man. You take out what you did not put in and reap what you did not sow."*

*His master replied, "I will judge you by your own words, you wicked servant! You knew, did you, that I am a hard man, taking out what I did not put in, and reaping what I did not sow? Why then didn't you put my money on deposit, so that when I came back, I could have collected it with interest?"*

*Then he said to those standing by, "'Take his mina away from him and give it to the one who has ten minas."*

*"Sir," they said, "he already has ten!"*

*He replied, "I tell you that to everyone who has, more will be given, but as for the one who has nothing, even what they have will be taken away. But those enemies of mine who did not want me to be king over them—bring them here and kill them in front of me.'"*

The greatest qualifier for leadership and other key responsibilities will be faithfulness to God right now.

Revelation 2:10,26—

*Do not be afraid of what you are about to suffer. I tell you, the devil will put some of you in prison to test you, and you will suffer persecution for ten days. Be faithful, even to the point of death, and I will give you life as your victor's crown…*

*To the one who is victorious and does my will to the end, **I will give authority over the nations.***

Revelation 3:11,21—

*I am coming soon. Hold on to what you have, so that no one will take your crown…*

*To the one who is victorious, **I will give the right to sit with me on my throne,** just as I was victorious and sat down with my Father on his throne.*

Revelation 4:10—

*… the twenty-four elders fall down before him who sits on the throne and worship him who lives for ever and ever. They lay their crowns before the throne…*

Revelation 5:9-10—

*And they sang a new song, saying: "You are worthy to take the scroll and to open its seals, because you were slain, and with your blood you purchased for God persons from every tribe and language and people and nation. You have made them to be a kingdom and priests to serve our God, and **they will reign on the earth.**"*

# OUR DESTINY— REINSTATED

| A. God's design | B. The Fall | C. Full restoration |
|---|---|---|
| WE WERE CREATED TO REIGN AND RELATE TO GOD | BUT, BEGIN READING IN GENESIS 1– NOT GENESIS 3 | RESTORED TO OUR RELATIONSHIP AND OUR ROLE |

# D. The Throne reveals much about our relationship with God.

**God's throne is referred to 40 times in Revelation.**

Randy Alcorn has expressed very well a summation which we should all consider.[29]

> *Revelation isn't primarily a book about the Antichrist or the Tribulation; it's a book about God reigning. He reigns over the fallen universe now, and He will reign uncontested over the new universe, with mankind reigning by his side.*

Alcorn goes further to quote Dr. Henry Grattan Guinness,

> *We must not regard this as a figure of speech, but as the description of an actual reality.*

Notice Jesus' words in Luke 12:32-34—

> *Do not be afraid, little flock, for **your father has been pleased to give you the Kingdom.** Sell your possessions and give to the poor. Provide purses for yourselves that will not wear out, a treasure in heaven that will never fail, where no thief comes near and no moth destroys. For where your treasure is, here your heart will be also.*

(We will study the throne more in lesson 11.)

**As we close this chapter, let's make three observations about the throne and reigning with Christ.**

1. The Kingdom transfer startles the imagination— and it is coming.

---

[29] *Heaven*, page 233

The profound nature of the Model Prayer, which is usually called the Lord's Prayer, highlights this.[30]

Matthew 6:9-13—

*This, then, is how you should pray:*

*Our father in heaven, hallowed be your name, your Kingdom come, your will be done, **on earth as it is in heaven**. Give us today our daily bread. And forgive us our debts, as we also have forgiven our debtors. And lead us not into temptation, but deliver us from the evil one. **For yours is the Kingdom and the power and the glory forever**. Amen*

Randy Alcorn reminds us—

*God has never abandoned His original plan that righteous human beings will inhabit and rule the earth…*

*Daniel 7:18 explicitly reveals that "saints of the Most High" will receive the Kingdom and will possess it forever.*[31]

Accordingly, the Kingdom will belong to God. The saints will steward it on His behalf— much as Adam and Eve were to steward Creation.

Daniel 7:27—

*Then the sovereignty, power and greatness of the kingdoms under **the whole heaven will be handed over to the Saints, the people of the Most High**. His Kingdom will be an everlasting Kingdom, and all rulers will worship and obey Him.*

---

[30] Our contention is that the Sermon on the Mount contains the "Model Prayer." This was, according to Luke, given to the disciples' request for Jesus to "teach them how to pray" (Luke 11:1ff.). It contains things Jesus would not need to request of the Father (i.e., forgiveness of sin). The Lord's Prayer, on the other hand, is found in John 17.

[31] *Heaven*, page 230

The rulers will be righteous and will be under the authority of Christ.

2. **Reigning in the future is a reward of service and the inheritance for faithfulness now.**

We must never serve God out of fleshly motives.

A good illustration application comes from athletes. If a person is truly an athlete that person does not just run for the trophy, but more so for the joy of the race, the discipline required, and the blessing that comes to one's heart.

Eric Liddell, the olympic runner after whom the famed film *Chariots of Fire* was made, said he sensed the smile of God as he ran.

This can be our approach to serving the Lord in every area of life now as we prepare to reign with Him in the future.

The parables Jesus shared indicated that the granting of responsibilities relates to diligent and faithful service. The Parable of the "Bags of Gold" and the "Sheep and the Goats" illustrate this (see Matthew 25:14-46).

Rejoicing is in order for those rewarded with service opportunities in God's Kingdom.

Matthew 5:12—

*Rejoice and be glad, for great is your reward in Heaven.*

Persons we can expect to be chosen for special opportunity are indicated clearly in Scripture.

Notice Matthew 5:1ff. (selected verses below from Matthew 5:3,5,8,10)—

*Blessed are the poor in spirit, for theirs is the Kingdom of heaven...*

*Blessed are the meek, for they will inherit the earth...*

*Blessed are the pure in heart for they will see God…*

*Blessed are those who are persecuted because of righteousness, for theirs is the Kingdom of heaven.*

3. **Along with thrones, crowns are the primary Biblical indicators of ruling.**

   We see crowds crowns throughout Revelation.

   Revelation 2:10—

   *Be faithful, even to the point of death, and I will give you life as your **victor's crown**.*

   Revelation 2:26—

   *To the one who is victorious and does my will to the end, I will give **authority over the nations**.*

   Revelation 3:11—

   *I am coming soon. Hold on to what you have, so that no one will take **your crow**n.*

   Revelation 3:21—

   *To Him who overcomes, **I will give the right to sit with me on my throne**, just as I overcame and sat down with my father on His throne.*

   Notice what happens with the crowns, though.

   Revelation 4:10—

   *The 24 elders fall down before Him who **sits on the throne**…*

   *They **lay their crowns** before the throne.*

In effect, it all comes from Jesus, it's all done for the glory of Jesus, and it all returns to Jesus.

David Jeremiah relates an old tale that points to this truth in *The Book of Signs*. [32]

> *Three men were crossing the desert by camel at night.*
>
> *A voice came out of the darkness: "Dismount. Pick up pebbles. Put them in your pockets. At the coming of the sun you will be both glad and sorry."*
>
> *When the sun came up the men reached into their pockets and pulled out not pebbles but diamonds.*
>
> *They were both glad and sorry. Glad they took as many as they did. Sorry they did not take more.*

God gives us opportunities.

Many…

Many…

Many opportunities.

---

[32] Jeremiah, *The Book of Signs*, page 203-204

# 5. Our Role in Ruling with Christ

116

# 6. Understanding the Millennium

**Main idea: Though there is some disagreement as to when the reign occurs and whether the 1,000 years is symbolic or literal, we can all agree: Jesus returns and reigns. Moreover, we will see a radical difference between His first coming and His return.**

*The Millennium question relates to whether the Old Earth will end after the return of Christ, or a thousand years later after the end of the Millennium.*

*— Randy Alcorn[33]*

## A. Three views on the Millennium

The compounding of the Latin word *mille*, which means "thousand," and *annum* which means "years," results in *millennium* which means "a thousand years."

The Millennium is a period of a thousand years which will occur when Jesus returns to Earth at the end of history to establish His earthly kingdom.

---

[33] *Heaven*, page 146

THE LATIN ROOTS

# MILLE + ANNUM = MILLENNIUM

# *1,000 YEARS*

## *THE 1,000 YEAR REIGN OF CHRIST'S EARTHLY KINGDOM*

The timing and the details of the Millennium have been studied and discussed for many years. That study and discussion will continue until Jesus returns in fulfillment of God's promises.

**Generally speaking, Christians hold to one of three views regarding the Millennium.** Postmillennial, premillennial, and amillennial views are often held quite adamantly by those who have studied the end times.

Without seeking to be simplistic, we should at least offer a few sentences about the postmillennial and amillennial viewpoints because more time will be spent on the premillennial approach.

**Note: each of these view points are based on *when* Christ returns—** and the question of whether He returns *after* "the 1,000 years" (i.e., He returns post-1,000 years, *post*-Millennium), whether He returns before "the 1,000 years" (i.e., He returns *pre*-Millennium), or at some other time.

1. **Postmillennial (Christ returns after the Millennium)**

The postmillennial viewpoint focuses on the Kingdom of Christ spreading throughout the world with God's justice ultimately prevailing across the earth before the return of Christ.

Following Christ's reign being established for a long duration (not necessarily a thousand years literally), Jesus will return to a significantly redeemed world.

2. **Amillennial (with the prefix *a*—, meaning "without," or "no" Millennium)**

The amillennial viewpoint focuses on the Millennium *not* being a literal thousand years. The events described in Revelation 20:3-7 are thought to be happening now with the Christian church reigning with Christ over the earth in victorious triumph empowered by the death and resurrection of Jesus. Many scholars including most Reformed theologians throughout Church History have held to this viewpoint.

3. **Premillennial (Christ returns before the Millennium)**

The premillennial viewpoint focuses on the Millennium as a literal thousand-year reign of Christ after His return when He defeats His enemies in the Battle of Armageddon.

God's promises of the Messiah's earthly reign will be fulfilled during the thousand-year time period. According to some teachings, the redeemed Jews will live in their homeland and the church will reign on earth with Christ. The Millennium will be concluded with a final rebellion. The Old Earth will be replaced by or transformed into the New Heaven and New Earth.

**POSTMILLENNIAL = JESUS RETURNS AFTER THE WORLD IMPROVES**

*1,000 YEAR "GOLDEN AGE" OF BETTERMENT, THEN...*  *CHRIST RETURNS*

**AMILLENNIAL = "WITHOUT," OR "NO" MILLENNIUM**

*NO LITERAL MILLENNIUM... EVERYTHING CHANGED FOR THE BETTER WITH HIS RESURRECTION* *CHRIST RETURNS*

**PREMILLENNIAL = CHRIST RETURNS BEFORE THE MILLENNIUM**

*CHRIST RETURNS* *HE DEFEATS HIS ENEMIES AND THEN SETS UP HIS RULE FOR 1,000 YEARS*

# B. Three truths to remember about each of these views.

### 1. They are each based on Scripture— on the same passage.

Revelation 20:3-7—

> He threw him into the Abyss, and locked and sealed it over him, to keep him from deceiving the nations anymore until the thousand years were ended. After that, he must be set free for a short time.
>
> I saw thrones on which were seated those who had been given authority to judge. And I saw the souls of those who had been beheaded because of their testimony about Jesus and because of the word of God. They

*had not worshiped the beast or its image and had not received its mark on their foreheads or their hands. They came to life and reigned with Christ a thousand years.*

*(The rest of the dead did not come to life until the thousand years were ended.)*

*This is the first resurrection. Blessed and holy are those who share in the first resurrection. The second death has no power over them, but they will be priests of God and of Christ and will reign with him for a thousand years.*

2.  **The difference in interpretation centers on when we reign with Christ, that is, how we view Revelation 20:7—**

    Revelation 20:7—

    *… they will be priests of God and of Christ and will reign with him for a thousand years.*

3.  **Our approach to the Millennium does not need to affect our view of the New Heaven and the New Earth.**

# C. A call for humility

There is some disagreement among a significant number of scholars and individual believers regarding the details in each of these viewpoints. Nonetheless, it is God who is in control, and everything will follow God's preordained plan.

Christians should approach these disagreements with humility, gentleness, and respect.

Regardless of how we view the Millennium, we can agree on the purposes of this reign of Christ.

# D. Four purposes of the Millennium

Why is there a period of 1,000 years inserted here in time instead of going directly into the eternal state? Why did God plan it that way?

Note: David Jeremiah, speaking from the premillennial viewpoint in *The Book of Signs*, has provided a helpful summation of the premillennial viewpoint which we will follow in this lesson.[34]

For some things we do not have an answer, but we can be sure that God's ways are perfect. He knows exactly what He is doing and why He is doing what He is doing. By considering the Word of God we can ascertain some purposes.

## 1. The Millennium will be a reward for the people of God.

We usually think of faithful work being rewarded by time off. We take vacations and days off and sabbaticals for needed replenishment and rest. Those are needed and appropriate and scripturally indicated.

However, in Matthew 25:23 we learn that God also offers a reward of MORE work, responsibility, and opportunity for jobs well done.

Matthew 25:23—

---

[34] These concepts and thoughts are further expressed on pages 364-377 of his book, *The Book of Signs*.

> *His master replied, "Well done, good and faithful servant! You have been faithful with a few things;* **I will put you in charge of many things. Come and share your master's happiness!"**

(Remember, as we learned in a previous lesson, it was God's original intention for us to reign with Him in the Garden.)

We will see new dimensions in those things as we have corresponding abilities, wisdom, and power to do any and all things that God places before us. We will be overflowing with joy to be serving alongside our Lord.

Notice the following passages of Scripture, as well.

Isaiah 40:10—

> *See, the Sovereign Lord comes with power, and he rules with a mighty arm.*
>
> *See,* **his reward is with him,** *and his recompense accompanies him.*

Matthew 16:27–

> *For the Son of Man is going to come in his Father's glory with his angels, and then* **he will reward each person according to what they have done.**

Matthew 25:34—

> *Then the King will say to those on his right, "Come, you who are blessed by my Father;* **take your inheritance, the kingdom prepared for you since the creation of the world."**

Revelation 22:12—

> *Look, I am coming soon!* **My reward is with me,** *and I will give to each person according to what they have done.*

2. **The Millennium will be a time of fulfillment of the prophetic pronouncements.**

   Jesus came the first time to redeem us, but the world rejected him. When He comes again He will rule the world in righteousness.

   God's covenant with David recorded in 2 Samuel 7:16 and the statement that Gabriel quoted to Mary in Luke 1:32-33 will be fulfilled.

   2 Samuel 7:16—

   > *Your house and your kingdom will endure forever before me;* ***your throne will be established forever.***

   Luke 1:32-33—

   > *He will be great and will be called the Son of the Most High.* ***The Lord God will give him the throne of his father David, and he will reign*** *over Jacob's descendants forever;* ***his kingdom will never end.***

   See also the following passages:

   Psalm 72:11—

   > *May all kings bow down to him and all nations serve him.*

   Isaiah 9:7–

   > *Of the greatness of his government and peace there will be no end.*
   >
   > *He will reign on David's throne and over his kingdom, establishing and upholding it with justice and righteousness from that time on and forever.*
   >
   > *The zeal of the Lord Almighty will accomplish this.*

   Isaiah 60:21—

*Then all your people will be righteous and they will possess the land forever.*

*They are the shoot I have planted, the work of my hands, for the display of my splendor.*

3. **The Millennium will provide the answer to the Model Prayer.**

We have learned the words to the Model Prayer and we have offered the prayer countless times. The fulfillment of that prayer will come when God's perfect will is done "on Earth as it is in Heaven."

Matthew 6:9-13—

*Our Father in heaven, hallowed be your name,*

***Your kingdom come, your will be done, on earth as it is in heaven.***

*Give us today our daily bread.*

*And forgive us our debts, as we also have forgiven our debtors.*

*And lead us not into temptation, but deliver us from the evil one.*

In fact, the words that some feel were additions to the prayer found in some late manuscripts will also come to fruition—

*For yours is the kingdom and the power and the glory forever.*

*Amen.*

4. **The Millennium will provide a demonstration of a better world still incomplete.**

There is an incredible ending following the Thousand Year Reign / Millennium. After Satan being bound for this extended period, he is released temporarily for one final rebellion.

Things are not yet perfect.

- Death will be *rare* during the Millennium.

- Sin will be *diminished* but possible.

- The human heart will *still be capable* of rebellion.

This is the final proof of the hopeless depravity of man apart from the grace of God. This happens after the Earth's population has experienced a thousand years of teaching and testimony and peace.

Yet, there is still that sinful nature leading up to the Great White Throne Judgment.

Revelation 20:7-15—

> When the thousand years are over, Satan will be released from his prison and will go out to deceive the nations in the four corners of the earth—Gog and Magog—and to gather them for battle. In number they are like the sand on the seashore. They marched across the breadth of the earth and surrounded the camp of God's people, the city he loves.

> But fire came down from heaven and devoured them. And the devil, who deceived them, was thrown into the lake of burning sulfur, where the beast and the false prophet had been thrown. They will be tormented day and night for ever and ever.

> Then I saw a great white throne and him who was seated on it. The earth and the heavens fled from his presence, and there was no place for them.

*And I saw the dead, great and small, standing before the throne, and books were opened. Another book was opened, which is the book of life. The dead were judged according to what they had done as recorded in the books.*

*The sea gave up the dead that were in it, and death and Hades gave up the dead that were in them, and each person was judged according to what they had done.*

*Then death and Hades were thrown into the lake of fire. The lake of fire is the second death.*

*Anyone whose name was not found written in the book of life was thrown into the lake of fire.*

## FOUR PURPOSES OF THE MILLENNIUM

1. Reward God's People

2. Prophetic Fulfillment

3. The Model Prayer

4. Demonstrate the Need

## E. What to expect during the Millennium

As we conclude this lesson, let's make five observations about what we might experience during the Millennium.

## 1. A time of peace will be experienced.

War will not be waged. Soldiers and sailors will not be deployed for combat.

Psalm 72:7—

*In his days may the righteous flourish and prosperity abound till the moon is no more.*

Micah 4:2-3—

*Many nations will come and say, "Come, let us go up to the mountain of the Lord, to the temple of the God of Jacob. He will teach us his ways, so that we may walk in his paths."*

*The law will go out from Zion, the word of the Lord from Jerusalem.*

*He will judge between many peoples and will settle disputes for strong nations far and wide.*

***They will beat their swords into plowshares and their spears into pruning hooks.*** *Nation will not take up sword against nation, nor will they train for war anymore.*

Even wild animals will not fight.

Isaiah 11:6-9—

*The wolf will live with the lamb, the leopard will lie down with the goat, the calf and the lion and the yearling together; and a little child will lead them.*

*The cow will feed with the bear, their young will lie down together, and the lion will eat straw like the ox.*

*The infant will play near the cobra's den, and the young child will put its hand into the viper's nest.*

*They will neither harm nor destroy on all my holy mountain, for the earth will be filled with the knowledge of the Lord as the waters cover the sea.*

## 2. Prosperity will be realized abundantly.

Healthy economic conditions will be known throughout the world.

Ezekiel 34:26-30—

*I will make them and the places surrounding my hill a blessing.*

*I will send down showers in season;* **there will be showers of blessing.** *The trees will yield their fruit and the ground will yield its crops; the people will be secure in their land.*

*They will know that I am the Lord, when I break the bars of their yoke and rescue them from the hands of those who enslaved them. They will no longer be plundered by the nations, nor will wild animals devour them. They will live in safety, and no one will make them afraid.*

*I will provide for them a land renowned for its crops, and they will no longer be victims of famine in the land or bear the scorn of the nations.*

*Then they will know that I, the Lord their God, am with them and that they, the Israelites, are my people, declares the Sovereign Lord.*

Amos 9:13—

*"The days are coming," declares the Lord, "when the reaper will be overtaken by the plowman and the planter by the one treading grapes. New wine will drip from the mountains and flow from all the hills..."*

3. **Purity will be the norm of life.**

   Sin will be diminished, and disobedience will be noted and dealt with.

   Isaiah 11:9–

   > *They will neither harm nor destroy on all my holy mountain, for the earth will be filled with the knowledge of the Lord as the waters cover the sea.*

   Isaiah 66:23—

   > *"From one New Moon to another and from one Sabbath to another, all mankind will come and bow down before me," says the Lord.*

   Zechariah 13:2—

   > *"On that day, I will banish the names of the idols from the land, and they will be remembered no more," declares the Lord Almighty.* **"I will remove... the spirit of impurity from the land."**

4. **Lifespans will be prolonged.**

   Some scholars suggest human longevity may return to pre-Flood durations.

   Isaiah 65:20—

   > *Never again will there be in it an infant who lives but a few days, or an old man who does not live out his years; the one who dies at a hundred will be thought a mere child; the one who fails to reach a hundred will be considered accursed.*

5. **Personal joy and contentment will be experienced in an era of happiness.**

Jesus will rule and reign on the Throne of David in the City of Jerusalem. The answer to the prayers of so many people who endure sadness and anguish now will be answered then.

# WHAT WE'LL EXPERIENCE

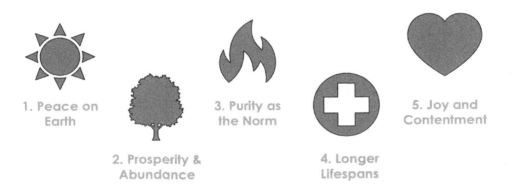

1. Peace on Earth

2. Prosperity & Abundance

3. Purity as the Norm

4. Longer Lifespans

5. Joy and Contentment

Notice what the Bible says about this point.

Isaiah 9:3—

> *You have enlarged the nation and increased their joy; they rejoice before you as people rejoice at the harvest, as warriors rejoice when dividing the plunder.*

Isaiah 12:3—

> *With joy you will draw water from the wells of salvation.*

Isaiah 14:7—

> *All the lands are at rest and at peace; they break into singing.*

Isaiah 25:8-9—

*He will swallow up death forever. The Sovereign Lord will wipe away the tears from all faces; he will remove his people's disgrace from all the earth. The Lord has spoken.*

*In that day they will say, "Surely this is our God; we trusted in him, and he saved us. This is the Lord, we trusted in him; let us rejoice and be glad in his salvation.*

# F. Comparing His first coming (with some rejection) with His return (and His reign)

We will see a significant difference in Christ's first coming and His return.

It is interesting to note that a song which is sung at Christmas as one of our most time-honored carols was not originally thought of as a Christmas carol but a song regarding our Lord's Return and the Golden Age to follow the Second Coming (i.e., Christ returns before— or pre— the 1,000 year reign, that is, Premillennium).

Notice the words based on Isaac Watts' interpretation of Psalm 98.

**Joy to the World**

*Joy to the world, the Lord is come!*
*Let earth receive her King;*
*Let every heart prepare Him room,*
*And heaven and nature sing,*
*And heaven and nature sing,*
*And heaven, and heaven, and nature sing.*

*Joy to the earth, the Savior reigns!*
*Let men their songs employ;*
*While fields and floods, rocks, hills and plains*
*Repeat the sounding joy,*
*Repeat the sounding joy,*
*Repeat, repeat, the sounding joy.*

*No more let sin and sorrow grow,*
*Nor thorns infest the ground;*
*He comes to make His blessing flow*
*Far as the curse is found,*
*Far as the curse is found,*
*Far as, far as, the curse is found.*

*He rules the world with truth and grace,*
*And makes the nations prove*
*The glories of His righteousness,*
*And wonders of His love,*
*And wonders of His love,*
*And wonders, wonders, of His love.*

*— Isaac Watts*

Those things did not happen at the time of Jesus' birth in Bethlehem.

- Earth did not receive her King or for the most part realize that He had come at all.

- The curse was not removed, and His rulership had not come to pass.

- The nations of the world did not acknowledge His righteousness or the wonders of His love.

These promises were not about His first coming. These things will be true when He returns the second time, and the Millennium reign occurs.

| First Coming | Second Coming |
| --- | --- |
| Swaddling cloths | Majestic purpose attire |
| Weary traveler | Untiring God |
| Nowhere to lay His head | Heir of all things |
| Rejected by tiny Israel | Acknowledged by every nation |
| Lovely Savior, acquainted with grief | Mighty God, anointed with gladness |
| Smitten with a reed | Ruling with a rod of iron |
| Wicked soldiers bowed in mockery | Every knee will bow + confess Lordship |
| Wore a crown of thorns | Will receive a crown of gold |
| Delivered up His Spirit in death | Now alive forevermore |
| Laid in a tomb | Will sit upon a throne |

# Part 3 — What Will Heaven Be Like?

# 7. The Old Passes (the New Heaven and the New Earth)

---

**Main idea: A New Heaven and a New Earth are coming— they're promised. Before they can arrive, though, the present Earth must pass.**

---

*People longed for a more perfect world.*

*We hear it in the dreams of the poets. We read it in literature. We see it in the paintings of the famous artists whose works fill the walls of the great museums of the world.*

*It's as if we instinctively understand that our paradise in the garden of Eden was the normal state of affairs for humanity, but we lost it after Adam and Eve sinned against God. Now we yearn for its restoration.*

*We want it back. We instinctively know things should be different.*

*We were made for a more perfect world.*

*— David Jeremiah*[35]

---

[35] *The Book of Signs,* pages 391-392

# A. Start with what's clear.

We must carefully and diligently read the Scriptures on all matters. Certain passages offer two incredible truths about our future.

1. **We know that something new is coming— a new heaven and a new earth.**

   Isaiah 65:17-19—

   > See, **I will create new heavens and a new earth.** The former things will not be remembered, nor will they come to mind.
   >
   > But be glad and rejoice forever in what I will create,
   > for I will create Jerusalem to be a delight and its people a joy.
   >
   > I will rejoice over Jerusalem and take delight in my people; the sound of weeping and of crying will be heard in it no more.

   Isaiah 66:22-23—

   > "As **the new heavens and the new earth that I make** will endure before me," declares the Lord, "so will your name and descendants endure. From one New Moon to another and from one Sabbath to another, all mankind will come and bow down before me," says the Lord.

2. **The old must pass away in order for the new to come.**

   2 Peter 3:7,10-13—

   > By the same word the present heavens and earth are reserved for fire, being kept for the day of judgment and destruction of the ungodly…

*But the day of the Lord will come like a thief. The heavens will disappear with a roar; the elements will be destroyed by fire, and the earth and everything done in it will be laid bare.*

*Since everything will be destroyed in this way, what kind of people ought you to be?*

*You ought to live holy and godly lives as you look forward to the day of God and speed its coming. That day will bring about the destruction of the heavens by fire, and the elements will melt in the heat. But in keeping with his promise we are looking forward to a new heaven and a new earth, where righteousness dwells.*

Hebrews 1:10-12—

*He also says, "In the beginning, Lord, you laid the foundations of the earth, and the heavens are the work of your hands. They will perish, but you remain; they will all wear out like a garment. You will roll them up like a robe; like a garment they will be changed. But you remain the same, and your years will never end."*

Psalm 102:25-27—

*In the beginning you laid the foundations of the earth, and the heavens are the work of your hands. They will perish, but you remain; they will all wear out like a garment. Like clothing you will change them and they will be discarded. But you remain the same, and your years will never end.*

Revelation 21-22—

*Then **I saw "a new heaven and a new earth,"** for the first heaven and the first earth had passed away, and there was no longer any sea.*

*I saw the Holy City, the new Jerusalem, coming down out of heaven from God, prepared as a bride beautifully dressed for her husband.*

*And I heard a loud voice from the throne saying, "Look! God's dwelling place is now among the people, and he will dwell with them. They will be* his people, and God himself will be with them and be their God. He will wipe every tear from their eyes. There will be no more death  or mourning or crying or pain, for the old order of things has passed away."

He who was seated on the throne said, **"I am making everything new!"** Then he said, "Write this down, for these words are trustworthy and true."

He said to me: "It is done. I am the Alpha and the Omega, the Beginning and the End. To the thirsty I will give water without cost from the spring of the water of life. Those who are victorious will inherit all this, and I will be their God and they will be my children. But the cowardly, the unbelieving, the vile, the murderers, the sexually immoral, those who practice magic arts, the idolaters and all liars—they will be consigned to the fiery lake of burning sulfur. This is the second death."

One of the seven angels who had the seven bowls full of the seven last plagues came and said to me, "Come, I will show you the bride, the wife of the Lamb."

And he carried me away in the Spirit to a mountain great and high, and showed me the Holy City, Jerusalem, coming down out of heaven from God.

It shone with the glory of God, and its brilliance was like that of a very precious jewel, like a jasper, clear as crystal. It had a great, high wall with twelve gates, and with twelve angels at the gates.

On the gates were written the names of the twelve tribes of Israel. There were three gates on the east, three on the north, three on the south and three on the west.

The wall of the city had twelve foundations, and on them were the names of the twelve apostles of the Lamb.

The angel who talked with me had a measuring rod of gold to measure the city, its gates and its walls. The city was laid out like a square, as long as it was wide. He measured the city with the rod and found it to be 12,000 stadia in length, and as wide and high as it is long.

The angel measured the wall using human measurement, and it was 144 cubits thick. The wall was made of jasper, and the city of pure gold, as pure as glass.

The foundations of the city walls were decorated with every kind of precious stone. The first foundation was jasper, the second sapphire, the third agate, the fourth emerald, the fifth onyx, the sixth ruby, the seventh chrysolite, the eighth beryl, the ninth topaz, the tenth turquoise, the eleventh jacinth, and the twelfth amethyst.

The twelve gates were twelve pearls, each gate made of a single pearl.

The great street of the city was of gold, as pure as transparent glass.

**I did not see a temple in the city, because the Lord God Almighty and the Lamb are its temple.** The city does not need the sun or the moon to shine on it, for the glory of God gives it light, and the Lamb is its lamp. The nations will walk by its light, and the kings of the earth will bring their splendor into it.

On no day will its gates ever be shut, for there will be no night there.

The glory and honor of the nations will be brought into it.

Nothing impure will ever enter it, nor will anyone who does what is shameful or deceitful, but only those whose names are written in the Lamb's book of life.


Then the angel showed me the river of the water of life, as clear as crystal, flowing from the throne of God and of the Lamb down the middle of the great street of the city.

*On each side of the river stood the tree of life, bearing twelve crops of fruit, yielding its fruit every month. And the leaves of the tree are for the healing of the nations.*

*No longer will there be any curse.*

*The throne of God and of the Lamb will be in the city, and his servants will serve him. They will see his face, and his name will be on their foreheads.*

*There will be no more night. They will not need the light of a lamp or the light of the sun, for the Lord God will give them light. And they will reign for ever and ever.*

*The angel said to me, "**These words are trustworthy and true**. The Lord, the God who inspires the prophets, sent his angel to show his servants the things that must soon take place."*

*"Look, I am coming soon! Blessed is the one who keeps the words of the prophecy written in this scroll."*

*I, John, am the one who heard and saw these things. And when I had heard and seen them, I fell down to worship at the feet of the angel who had been showing them to me.*

*But he said to me, "Don't do that! I am a fellow servant with you and with your fellow prophets and with all who keep the words of this scroll. Worship God!"*

*Then he told me, "Do not seal up the words of the prophecy of this scroll, because the time is near. Let the one who does wrong continue to do wrong; let the vile person continue to be vile; let the one who does right continue to do right; and let the holy person continue to be holy."*

*"**Look, I am coming soon! My reward is with me**, and I will give to each person according to what they have done. I am the Alpha and the Omega, the First and the Last, the Beginning and the End. Blessed are those who wash their robes, that they may have the right to the tree of life and may go through the gates into the city. Outside are the dogs, those who practice magic arts, the sexually immoral, the murderers, the idolaters and everyone who loves and practices falsehood. I, Jesus, have sent my angel to give you this testimony for the churches. I am the Root and the Offspring of David, and the bright Morning Star."*

*The Spirit and the bride say, "Come!"*

*And let the one who hears say, "Come!"*

*Let the one who is thirsty come; and let the one who wishes take the free gift of the water of life.*

*I warn everyone who hears the words of the prophecy of this scroll: If anyone adds anything to them, God will add to that person the plagues described in this scroll.*

*And if anyone takes words away from this scroll of prophecy, God will take away from that person any share in the tree of life and in the Holy City, which are described in this scroll.*

*He who testifies to these things says, **"Yes, I am coming soon."***

*Amen.*

*Come, Lord Jesus.*

*The grace of the Lord Jesus be with God's people.*

*Amen.*

3.  This leads us to an obvious question: when will the fulfillment of this promise occur? When does the "new come" and the "old pass"?

    In his *Book of Signs*, David Jeremiah proposes a timeline.[36]

    > *After the rapture of the Church, the seven years of tribulation, the Battle of Armageddon, the return of Christ, the Millennium, and the Great White Throne Judgment, God will draw the curtains on human history, and the entire universe will undergo a purifying conflagration.*

    > *All evidence of disease will be burned up. All evidence of disobedience will melt away. All the remnants and results of sin, sorrow, and suffering will be destroyed.*

    > *Out of the smoldering ruins, God will recreate all physical reality, and He will bring forth a fresh universe— a New Heaven and a New Earth.*

4.  Below we will evaluate the new that is coming— at the of this lesson and more in-depth in the following lesson— let's begin with what is passing.

# B. What does the Scripture mean that "heaven and earth will pass away"?

Some scholars believe and teach that the current universe will be totally annihilated and completely destroyed, while others interpret 2 Peter 3:10,12 and Revelation 21:1-5 somewhat differently.

---

[36] David Jeremiah, *Book of Signs*, page 400.

2 Peter 3:10,12—

> *But the day of the Lord will come like a thief. The heavens will disappear with a roar; the elements will be destroyed by fire, and the earth and everything done in it will be laid bare.*
>
> *Since everything will be destroyed in this way, what kind of people ought you to be? You ought to live holy and godly lives as you look forward to the day of God and speed its coming. That day will bring about the destruction of the heavens by fire, and the elements will melt in the heat.*

See Revelation 21:1-5 (the entire chapter was quoted just a few pages ago).

The phrases "burned up" or "laid bare or exposed" and "pass away" and "new"— which are featured throughout these passages— are keys to understanding what the Scripture means.

Strong clues are also helpful when we consider the transition from the old creation to the new creation in 2 Peter 3:5-7 and 1 Corinthians 15. That is, we can look at the flood in Noah's day, the resurrection of the body, and the victory over death.

1.   **What we see in the flood in Noah's day (2 Peter 3:5-7)**

2 Peter 3:5-7—

> *But they deliberately forget that long ago **by God's word** the heavens came into being and the earth was formed out of water and by water. By these waters also the world of that time was deluged and destroyed. **By the same word the present heavens and earth are reserved for fire, being kept for the day of judgment and destruction of the ungodly.***

2.   **What we see in the resurrection of the body (1 Corinthians 15)**

1 Corinthians 15:35-50—

*But someone will ask, "How are the dead raised? With what kind of body will they come?"*

*How foolish! What you sow does not come to life unless it dies.*

*When you sow, you do not plant the body that will be, but just a seed, perhaps of wheat or of something else…*

*So will it be with the resurrection of the dead. The body that is sown is perishable, **it is raised imperishable**; it is sown in dishonor, it is **raised in glory**; it is sown in weakness, it is raised in power; it is sown a natural body, it is raised a spiritual body.*

*If there is a natural body, **there is also a spiritual body.***

*So it is written: "The first man Adam became a living being"; the last Adam, a life-giving spirit.*

*The spiritual did not come first, but the natural, and after that the spiritual. The first man was of the dust of the earth; the second man is of heaven. As was the earthly man, so are those who are of the earth; and as is the heavenly man, so also are those who are of heaven. And just as we have borne the image of the earthly man, so shall we bear the image of the heavenly man.*

*I declare to you, brothers and sisters, that flesh and blood cannot inherit the kingdom of God, nor does the perishable inherit the imperishable.*

## 3.   What we see in victory over death (1 Corinthians 15)

1 Corinthians 15:51-58—

*Listen, I tell you a mystery: We will not all sleep, but **we will all be changed**— in a flash, in the twinkling of an eye, at the last trumpet. For the trumpet will sound, the dead will be raised imperishable, and we will be changed. **For the perishable must clothe itself with the*** *imperishable, and the mortal with immortality.* *When the perishable has been clothed with the imperishable, and the mortal with immortality, then the saying that is written will come true: "Death has been swallowed up in victory."*

*Where, O death, is your victory?*

*Where, O death, is your sting?*

*The sting of death is sin, and the power of sin is the law. But thanks be to God! He gives us the victory through our Lord Jesus Christ.*

*Therefore, my dear brothers and sisters, stand firm. Let nothing move you. Always give yourselves fully to the work of the Lord, because you know that your labor in the Lord is not in vain.*

4.  **What we see from words and phrases featured throughout these passages.**

    - **Burned up**

      This phrase literally means "laid bare" or "exposed."

      The Greek word used by Peter conveys the idea of being laid open or uncovered for exposure. This is not so much utter destruction but **a stripping of everything away and returning to the original elements —a purification time** of removing everything having to do with sin, death, and earthliness in its fallen condition.

    - **New**

      Two Greek words apply to the term "new."

      *Neos* denotes to replace the old with the same like it. For instance, you might purchase a new pair of shoes— because the old are worn out.

*Kainos* has to do with quality— it is **superior and totally unlike the thing it replaces** (i.e., a butterfly is so superior to a caterpillar that there's no indication the latter ever was the former).

John used the second term throughout Revelation which means not so much utter destruction but rather total transformation.

(Paul uses the same term to emphasize how "new" we are in Christ, as well, in 2 Corinthians 5:17.)

- **Pass away**

The Greek word does not mean to cease to exist but **to change.** The idea is the passing from one state to another.

Consider the terms we use when loved ones die. They pass away not in the sense of ceasing to exist, but they have moved from one state to another— a better one.

- **Like the Flood**

There is a strong suggestion of the transition from the "old creation" depicted in Noah's day to the "new creation" that followed the Great Flood.

God did not obliterate the earth in the days of Noah but He definitely renovated it. At the end of the age the transition will be more extensive and miraculous.

The words "transformed", "imperishable", and "fit for eternity" are appropriate.

(See 2 Peter 3:5-7 above under point 1.)

- **Like the resurrection of the body**

The process of this "newness" can be seen as a parallel to resurrection of the human body. The "new" will be the sense of quality or essence not in the sense of time.

We studied the importance of Jesus' Resurrection and what it reveals about our future state in chapter 4.)

• **Victory over death**

David Jeremiah confesses, "I don't believe God intends to give Satan the satisfaction of having irreparably ruined the divine creation of Genesis 1:31. God did not abandon His creation. He will restore it to His perfect and original intention. Satan did not win!"[37]

## C. The principles of the New Heaven and the New Earth— what's coming.

David Jeremiah also writes of the change that's coming.[38]

*When this new creation is finished and God has purified it, it is still the same earth and still the same heaven, but it will have been purged. It will be made fresh. All the stains of sin will be gone. All the evidences of death. All the signs of disease.*

Notably, the New Heaven and New Earth has a few striking features— each of which stand in stark contrast to "earth now."

---

[37] Jeremiah, *The Book of Signs*, page 399

[38] *Signs*, page 400

1.  **The removal of the sea = no more separation between people and groups.**

    The Bible does not say that there will be *no* beautiful bodies of water.

    When one considers the composition of planet Earth (and also the composition of our glorified bodies that are so superior), we must remind ourselves that the surface of earth is 71% water and oceans. Those bodies of water called oceans and seas with salt content are not inhabitable by humans.

    God could redesign and perhaps restore the bodies of water to freshness. We can be sure that barriers such as the barrier the sea has been will no longer be a separator or terror producing hindrance. God has inspired the statement regarding the sea and His Word is without error— even if we don't fully yet understand it.

    > Revelation 21:1—
    >
    > > *.... the first heaven and the first earth had passed away, and **there was no longer any sea.***

2.  **The reversal of the curse of the Fall = no more causes of pain, no reminders of it.**

    The original "curse" means mankind has lived a self-inflicted uphill battle throughout the course of human history.

    In the midst of the challenges, decay, deterioration, breakdowns, failures, droughts, fires, floods, tornadoes, and hurricanes we see the effects of sin.

    This will suddenly change.

    And when it does, it will transform completely.

Genesis 3:17-19—

> To Adam he said, "Because you listened to your wife and ate fruit from the tree about which I commanded you, 'You must not eat from it,' **cursed is the ground because of you**; through painful toil you will eat food from it all the days of your life. It will produce thorns and thistles for you, and you will eat the plants of the field. By the sweat of your brow you will eat your food until you return to the ground, since from it you were taken; for dust you are and to dust you will return."

Revelation 22:3—

> **No longer will there be any curse.** The throne of God and of the Lamb will be in the city, and his servants will serve him.

3. **Notably, everything is restored in the New Heaven and New Earth.**

Revelation 21:4-5—

> He will wipe every tear from their eyes. There will be no more death or mourning or crying or pain, for the old order of things has passed away.
>
> He who was seated on the throne said, **"I am making everything new!"**
>
> Then he said, "Write this down, for these words are trustworthy and true."

Romans 8:18-27—

> I consider that our present sufferings are not worth comparing with **the glory that will be revealed in us.** For the creation waits in eager **expectation for the children of God to be revealed.**
>
> For the creation was subjected to frustration, not by its own choice, but by the will of the one who subjected it, in hope that **the creation itself**

*will be liberated from its bondage to decay and brought into the freedom and glory of the children of God.*

*We know that the whole creation has been groaning as in the pains of childbirth right up to the present time. Not only so, but we ourselves, who have the firstfruits of the Spirit, groan inwardly as we wait eagerly for our adoption to sonship, the redemption of our bodies. For in this hope we were saved.*

*But hope that is seen is no hope at all.*

*Who hopes for what they already have?*

*But if we hope for what we do not yet have, we wait for it patiently.*

*In the same way, the Spirit helps us in our weakness. We do not know what we ought to pray for, but the Spirit himself intercedes for us through wordless groans.*

*And he who searches our hearts knows the mind of the Spirit, because the Spirit intercedes for God's people in accordance with the will of God.*

# D. A supernatural encounter— that's both an ending and a new beginning

**In other words, when we encounter the New Heaven and New Earth we will experience everything we've longed to understand about God.**

Furthermore, that experience will be permanent.

This leads to the follow-up question, what will this experience be like?

This will be the subject of the following lesson.

# 8. The New Comes (the New Heaven and the New Earth)

---

**Main idea: Scripture describes the New Heaven and New Earth— what is coming— as both a country and a city. This is the place of our true citizenship.**

---

*Heaven is God's home. Earth is our home. Jesus Christ, as the God-man, forever links God and mankind, and thereby forever links Heaven and earth.*

*As Ephesians 1:10 demonstrates, this idea of earth and Heaven becoming one is explicitly Biblical. Christ will make earth into Heaven and Heaven into earth.*

*Just as the wall that separates God and mankind is torn down in Jesus, so too the wall that separates Heaven and earth will be forever demolished. There will be one universe, with all things in Heaven and on earth together under One Head, Jesus Christ.*

*— Randy Alcorn*[39]

---

[39] *Heaven*, page 103

# A. Two terms help us comprehend Heaven

What are the descriptive details of this remarkable place we will dwell with God forever?

1. **Scripture describes Heaven as a country.**

   Luke 19:12—

   > He said: "A man of noble birth **went to a distant country** to have himself appointed king and then to return."

   Hebrews 11:14-16—

   > People who say such things show that they are looking for a country of their own. If they had been thinking of the country they had left, they would have had opportunity to return. Instead, **they were longing for a better country—a heavenly one.** Therefore God is not ashamed to be called their God, for he has prepared a city for them.

2. **Scripture describes Heaven as a city.**

   Hebrews 12:22-23,28, and 13:12-14—

   > But you have come to Mount Zion, to **the city of the living God, the heavenly Jerusalem**. You have come to thousands upon thousands of angels in joyful assembly, to the church of the firstborn, whose names are written in heaven.

   > Therefore, since we are receiving a kingdom that cannot be shaken, let us be thankful, and so worship God acceptably with reverence and awe…

*And so Jesus also suffered outside the city gate to make the people holy through his own blood. Let us, then, go to him outside the camp, bearing the disgrace he bore.* **For here we do not have an enduring city, but we are looking for the city that is to come.**

Revelation 21-22 (fifteen times)— the full citation of this passage is located in Chapter 7, section A-2 of this book.

Our understanding of what a city is involves buildings, streets, residences, people, activities, events, gatherings, education, entertainment, activities, and religion.

**In the next section of this lesson we will explore what "the country" of Heaven is like. Then, in the following section we'll evaluate the "city." Finally, we'll make the most important observation of all.**

# B. God's country / nation / kingdom

Years ago many of us learned the song *Do Lord.*

*I've got a home in glory land, that outshines the sun*
*I've got a home in glory land, that outshines the sun*
*I've got a home in glory land, that outshines the sun*
*Look away beyond the blue.*

*Do Lord, oh, do Lord, oh, do remember me,*
*Do Lord, oh, do Lord, oh, do remember me,*
*Do Lord, oh, do Lord, oh, do remember me,*
*Look away beyond the blue.*

*I took Jesus as my Savior, you take Him too,*
*I took Jesus as my Savior, you take Him too,*

*I took Jesus as my Savior, you take Him too,*
*Look away beyond the blue.*

*Do Lord, oh, do Lord, oh, do remember me,*
*Do Lord, oh, do Lord, oh, do remember me,*
*Do Lord, oh, do Lord, oh, do remember me,*
*Look away beyond the blue.*

*I read about it in the book of Revelation, you read it, too*
*I read about it in the book of Revelation, you read it, too*
*I read about it in the book of Revelation, you read it, too*
*Look away beyond the blue.*

*Do Lord, oh, do Lord, oh, do remember me,*
*Do Lord, oh, do Lord, oh, do remember me,*
*Do Lord, oh, do Lord, oh, do remember me,*
*Look away beyond the blue.*

*—Bill Black*

Consider the promises of Heaven.

No darkness, no night, no crime, no evil, no pain, no distress, no regrets, and on and on and on…

The glory of God will fill the New Heaven and the New Earth with perfect truth, righteousness, and perfected relationships enduring throughout eternity.

Paul Enns offers a worthy summary outline, which makes seven observations about the New Heaven and New Earth— about what the "country" or "kingdom" of Heaven is like.[40]

After reviewing these seven we will talk more about the "city."

---

[40] See *Heaven Revealed*, pages 109-119

1.  ## The glory of God will fill the earth.

    God's Glory will illuminate the New Heaven and the New Earth with brilliance far outshining the sun.

    Revelation 21:23—

    > The city does not need the sun or the moon to shine on it, for **the glory of God gives it light, and the Lamb is its lamp.**

    Ezekiel 43:2—

    > ... and I saw the glory of the God of Israel coming from the east. His voice was like the roar of rushing waters, and **the land was radiant with his glory.**

    Isaiah 60:1-3—

    > Arise, shine, for your light has come, and **the glory of the Lord rises upon you.**

    > See, darkness covers the earth and thick darkness is over the peoples, but the Lord rises upon you and his glory appears over you.

    > **Nations will come to your light, and kings to the brightness of your dawn.**

2.  ## The New Earth will be like Eden.

    Eden was unstained and untouched by sin until a choice was made by Adam that required banishment.

    Christ, the Last Adam, will restore the earth and Eden to their condition prior to the Fall of man.

    Genesis 2:8-14—

*Now the Lord God had planted a garden in the east, in Eden; and there he put the man he had formed. The Lord God made all kinds of trees grow out of the ground—trees that were pleasing to the eye and good for food.*

***In the middle of the garden were the tree of life and the tree of the knowledge of good and evil.***

*A river watering the garden flowed from Eden; from there it was separated into four headwaters.*

*The name of the first is the Pishon; it winds through the entire land of Havilah, where there is gold.*

*(The gold of that land is good; aromatic resin and onyx are also there.)*

*The name of the second river is the Gihon; it winds through the entire land of Cush.*

*The name of the third river is the Tigris; it runs along the east side of Ashur.*

*And the fourth river is the Euphrates.*

Isaiah 51:3—

*The Lord will surely comfort Zion and will look with compassion on all her ruins; **he will make her deserts like Eden, her wastelands like the garden of the Lord**. Joy and gladness will be found in her, thanksgiving and the sound of singing.*

## 3. The Tree of Life will be on Earth.

The Tree of Life was one of the predominant features in the Garden of Eden.

Genesis 2:15-17—

*The Lord God took the man and put him in the Garden of Eden to work it and take care of it.*

*And the Lord God commanded the man, "You are free to eat from any tree in the garden; but you must not eat from the tree of the knowledge of good and evil, for when you eat from it you will certainly die."*

God placed the Tree of Life and the Tree of the Knowledge of Good and Evil in the midst of the Garden of Eden. God gave a clear command regarding the Tree of Knowledge of Good and Evil.

The freedom of choice was an indicator of mankind being created in God's image. Then, man's decision to disobey God resulted in the fall of man and the fall of this perfect creation of God.

After the Fall, Adam and Eve were removed from the Garden— and from the presence of the Tree of Life.

Genesis 3:22-24—

*And the Lord God said, "The man has now become like one of us, knowing good and evil. He must not be allowed to reach out his hand and **take also from the tree of life and eat, and live forever**."*

*So the Lord God banished him from the Garden of Eden to work the ground from which he had been taken.*

*After he drove the man out, **he placed on the east side of the Garden of Eden cherubim and a flaming sword flashing back and forth to guard the way to the tree of life**.*

We see mankind living near the Tree of Life in the New Heaven / New Earth.

The situation that resulted from the choice of man to willfully disobey God has now been resolved. The inhabitants of the New Heaven/New Earth have been qualified to reside there forever. The Tree of Life from which they had been banished is readily available.

Revelation 22:1-3a,14—

> Then the angel showed me the river of the water of life, as clear as crystal, flowing from the throne of God and of the Lamb down the middle of the great street of the city.
>
> **On each side of the river stood the tree of life**, bearing twelve crops of fruit, yielding its fruit every month. **And the leaves of the tree are for the healing of the nations**.
>
> No longer will there be any curse...
>
> Blessed are those who wash their robes, that they may have the right to the tree of life and may go through the gates into the city.

Erwin Lutzer details why Adam and Eve had to be removed from the Tree of Life.[41] In a word, it was *grace* that evicted them.

> If Adam and Eve had eaten of the other special tree of the garden— the tree of life— they would have been immortalized in their sinful condition. They never would have qualified for the heaven that God wanted them to enjoy.

With the curse of sin removed and its subsequent issues resolved, man can now live near the Tree.

## 4. The River of Life will flow forever.

The River of Life ran through the middle of Eden, flowing presumably to the ends of the earth. Likewise, we see the River featured in the New Heaven / New Earth.

Genesis 2:10—

---

[41] See his book *One Minute After You Die* (page 44).

> ***A river watering the garden flowed from Eden;*** *from there it was separated into four headwaters.*

Revelation 22:1-2b—

> ***Then the angel showed me the river of the water of life****, as clear as crystal, flowing from the throne of God and of the Lamb down the middle of the great street of the city.*
>
> *On each side of the river stood the tree of life, bearing twelve crops of fruit, yielding its fruit every month. And the leaves of the tree are for the healing of the nations.*

What is the meaning of the River of Life?

The waters of the River will be literal while reflecting and implying spiritual blessings—power, purity, eternal life.

## 5. The deserts will gush with water.

Water is essential for physical life and living water is essential for spiritual life. Both will be abundant in the New Heaven and New Earth.

> Isaiah 35:6-7—

> *Then will the lame leap like a deer, and the mute tongue shout for joy.*
>
> ***Water will gush forth in the wilderness and streams in the desert.***
>
> *The burning sand will become a pool, the thirsty ground bubbling springs.*
>
> *In the haunts where jackals once lay, grass and reeds and papyrus will grow.*

Isaiah 41:18—

> **I will make rivers flow** on barren heights, and springs within the valleys. **I will turn the desert into pools of water**, and the **parched ground into springs**.

### 6. A beautiful and bountiful land will flourish.

Joel 2:23–

> Be glad, people of Zion, rejoice in the Lord your God, for he has given you the autumn rains because he is faithful.
>
> He sends you abundant showers, both autumn and spring rains, as before.

Joel 3:18—

> In that day the mountains will drip new wine, and the hills will flow with milk; all the ravines of Judah will run with water.
>
> A fountain will flow out of the Lord's house and will water the valley of acacias.

Ezekiel 34:27—

> The trees will yield their fruit and the ground will yield its crops; the people will be secure in their land. **They will know that I am the Lord, when I break the bars of their yoke and rescue them from the hands of those who enslaved them**.

Isaiah 30:23–

> He will also send you rain for the seed you sow in the ground, and the food that comes from the land will be rich and plentiful. In that day your cattle will graze in broad meadows.

Isaiah 65:21—

> *They will build houses and dwell in them; they will plant vineyards and eat their fruit.*
>
> ***The land will be both beautiful and productive.*** *There will be no diseases, insects, droughts, or floods to hinder the crops.*

7. **Animals will be plentiful and peaceful.**

Many people who love animals wonder whether there will be animals in the New Heaven and Earth.[42]

> *Because God has a future plan for both mankind and Earth, it strongly suggests that He has a future plan for animals as well.*

His statement seems Scripturally sound.

Isaiah 11:6-9–

> *The **wolf will live with the lamb**, the leopard will lie down with the goat, the calf and the lion and the yearling together; and a little child will lead them.*
>
> *The cow will feed with the bear, their young will lie down together, and the lion will eat straw like the ox.*
>
> *The **infant will play near the cobra's den, and the young child will put its hand into the viper's nest**.*
>
> *They will neither harm nor destroy on all my holy mountain, for **the earth will be filled with the knowledge of the Lord as the waters cover the sea**.*

Isaiah 65:25—

---

42 Randy Alcorn, *Heaven*, page 388

*"The wolf and the lamb will feed together, and the lion will eat straw like the ox, and dust will be the serpent's food. They will neither harm nor destroy on all my holy mountain," says the Lord.*

Humans and animals share uniqueness in that both are living beings. While humans are created in the image of God, animals are not. However, they do seem destined for redemption.

Remember, God saved them through the Flood in the days of Noah.

Genesis 9:9-17—

*"I now establish my covenant with you and with your descendants after you and with every living creature that was with you—the birds, the livestock and all the wild animals, all those that came out of the ark with you—every living creature on earth. I establish my covenant with you: Never again will all life be destroyed by the waters of a flood; never again will there be a flood to destroy the earth."*

*And God said, "This is the sign of the **covenant I am making between me and you and every living creature with you,** a covenant for all generations to come: I have set my rainbow in the clouds, and it will be the sign of the covenant between me and the earth. Whenever I bring clouds over the earth and the rainbow appears in the clouds, **I will remember my covenant between me and you and all living creatures of every kind.** Never again will the waters become a flood to destroy all life. Whenever the rainbow appears in the clouds, **I will see it and remember the everlasting covenant between God and all living creatures of every kind on the earth."***

*So God said to Noah, **"This is the sign of the covenant I have established between me and all life on the earth."***

God brought judgment by water followed by the promise to never again utilize a flood to destroy all flesh. So then, we may expect the reality of judgment by fire in possibly a similar catastrophic action.

In addition, Heaven isn't just described as a "country" but as a "city," the Holy City— the New Jerusalem.

# C. The Holy City, the New Jerusalem— the "city of cities"

**The Book of Revelation offers the most detailed picture of the remarkable City of Cities.** John quotes Jesus— from his vision— the first time he writes of the city.

> Revelation 3:12—
>
> *The one who is victorious I will make a pillar in the temple of my God. Never again will they leave it. I will write on them the name of my God and the name of **the city of my God, the new Jerusalem, which is coming down out of heaven from my God**; and I will also write on them my new name.*

**Later in Revelation, John continues to tell us of the creation of the New Heaven and the New Earth, and then— we're told— the great city of new Jerusalem will descend from the sky and will become the capital city of God's eternal Kingdom.**

We should realize that—

- The City of Jerusalem is not actually the entire New Heaven and New Earth in and of itself.

- The Holy City is the capital of Heaven.

**Notice how the City is described as it descends from John's account.**

Revelation 21:1-5—

> Then I saw "a new heaven and a new earth," for the first heaven and the first earth had passed away, and there was no longer any sea.
>
> **I saw the Holy City, the new Jerusalem, coming down out of heaven from God, prepared as a bride beautifully dressed for her husband.**
>
> And I heard a loud voice from the throne saying, "Look! God's dwelling place is now among the people, and he will dwell with them. They will be his people, and God himself will be with them and be their God. He will wipe every tear from their eyes. There will be no more death or mourning or crying or pain, for the old order of things has passed away."
>
> He who was seated on the throne said, "I am making everything new!"
>
> Then he said, "Write this down, for these words are trustworthy and true."

**John seems to clearly indicate that the City has already been built and is coming down out of the highest Heaven**. In other words, the New Jerusalem is an actual, existing, physical city presently located within the 3rd Heaven.

Jesus referred to New Jerusalem as the "City of My God" in Revelation 3:12. Evidently this is the City wherein Jesus is preparing for us a place.

Here are seven features of the Holy City.

## 1. The City is massive.

According to Revelation 21:15-16 the exact dimensions of the city that was laid out in a square were 12,000 stadia in length, in width, and in height. That is the equivalent of 1,400 miles.

Revelation 21:15-16—

*The angel who talked with me had a measuring rod of gold to measure the city, its gates and its walls. The city was laid out like a square, as long as it was wide. He measured the city with the rod and found it to be 12,000 stadia in length, and as wide and high as it is long.*

It is possible that these dimensions have symbolic importance. They also may be regarded, however, as literal. In verse 17 the measurements emphasizes that they are given using "man's measurement."

J.B. Smith defines the size and scope of this city.[43]

*If you compare the New Jerusalem to the United States, you would measure from the Atlantic Ocean coastline and westward, it would mean a city from the furthest Maine to the furthest Florida, and from the shore of the Atlantic to Colorado.*

*And from the United States Pacific Coast eastward, it would cover the United States as far as the Mississippi River, with the line extending north through Chicago and continuing on the West Coast of Lake Michigan, up to the Canadian border.[44]*

Randy Alcorn also shares interesting thoughts about the possible size of the New Jerusalem:

*Given the dimensions of a 1400-mile cube, if the City consisted of different levels (we don't know this), and if each story were a generous 12 feet high, the City could have over 600,000 stories.*

*If they were on different levels, billions of people could occupy the new Jerusalem, with many square miles per person.*

---

[43] Quoted by Randy Alcorn in *Heaven*, page 251

[44] Quoted by David Jeremiah, *Signs*, page 409.

2. **The twelve gates of pearl, opening to the vast, high, broad wall.**

    Revelation 21:12—

    > *It had a great, high wall with twelve gates… On the gates were written the names of the twelve tribes…*

    Revelation 21:17-18—

    > *The angel measured the wall using human measurement, and it was 144 cubits thick. The wall was made of jasper, and the city of pure gold, as pure as glass.*

3. **The foundations, whose Architect and Builder is God.**

    The foundations are mentioned in Revelation 21, as well as Hebrews 11 (which recounts the pursuit of Abraham).

    Revelation 21:14,19-21—

    > *The wall of the city had twelve foundations, and on them were the names of the twelve apostles of the Lamb.*

    > *The foundations of the city walls were decorated with every kind of precious stone. The first foundation was jasper, the second sapphire, the third agate, the fourth emerald, the fifth onyx, the sixth ruby, the seventh chrysolite, the eighth beryl, the ninth topaz, the tenth turquoise, the eleventh jacinth, and the twelfth amethyst. The twelve gates were twelve pearls, each gate made of a single pearl.*

    > *The great street of the city was of gold, as pure as transparent glass.*

    Hebrews 11:10—

    > *For he was looking forward to the city with foundations, whose architect and builder is God.*

Evidently these things were and are important in reference to the City of God.

4.  **Streets constructed of gold.**

    The reference in Revelation 21:21 to uniquely golden streets made of gold that is like transparent glass adds to the description of the astounding physical beauty of the Holy City.

    > Revelation 21:21—
    >
    > *The twelve gates were twelve pearls, each gate made of a single pearl. **The great street of the city was of gold, as pure as transparent glass**.*

    This is one of the most "famous" features of the Holy City.

5.  **The Tree of Life.**

    Revelation 22:2 highlights a striking feature of the City we studied earlier.

    The tree is mentioned 3 times in Genesis 2 and 4 times in Revelation, 3 of which are in this chapter.

    In Revelation 2:7 we learn that the tree of life is now in Paradise, the Present or Intermediate Heaven, awaiting the time of the relocation to the New Heaven and the New Earth.

    > Revelation 2:7—
    >
    > *Whoever has ears, let them hear what the Spirit says to the churches. To the one who is victorious, **I will give the right to eat from the tree of life**, which is in the paradise of God.*

    Here are the references from Revelation 22.

Revelation 22:1-2—

> Then the angel showed me the river of the water of life, as clear as crystal, flowing from the throne of God and of the Lamb down the middle of the great street of the city. On each side of the river stood the tree of life, bearing twelve crops of fruit, yielding its fruit every month. **And the leaves of the tree are for the healing of the nations.**

Revelation 22:14—

> Blessed are those who wash their robes, that **they may have the right to the tree of life...**

Revelation 22:19—

> And if anyone takes words away from this scroll of prophecy, God will take away from that person any **share in the tree of life and in the Holy City**, which are described in this scroll.

A respected scholar indicates that the term "tree of life" could be a collective term like *avenue* and *river*— meaning multiple trees not just one.[45]

Who knows? God is in charge of all things. We will see.

6.  **The pure river of the water of life.**

Notice again Revelation 22:1-2 along with Psalm 46:4. This indeed will be the most beautiful and beneficial river of time and eternity. The importance of water as an essential element of life continues to be a vital part of human life. This city truly merits the position of the river at the center of human life.

Revelation 22:1-2—

---

[45] Alcorn cites William Hendricksen in *Heaven* page 258.

*Then the angel showed me the river of **the water of life, as clear as crystal, flowing from the throne of God** and of the Lamb down the middle of the great street of the city. On each side of the river stood the tree of life, bearing twelve crops of fruit, yielding its fruit every month. And the leaves of the tree are for the healing of the nations.*

Psalm 46:4—

*There is **a river whose streams make glad the city of God**, the holy place where the Most High dwells.*

7. **The main characteristic of this City is Holiness.**

This will be a holy place for people made holy by the blood of Jesus. Since there will be no sin, there will be no courtrooms, no jails, no prisons, no hospitals, or funeral homes.

Revelation 21:2,10—

*I saw **the Holy City**, the new Jerusalem, coming down out of heaven from God, prepared **as a bride beautifully dressed for her husband…***

*And he carried me away in the Spirit to a mountain great and high, and showed me **the Holy City**, Jerusalem, coming down out of heaven from God.*

# D. The most important feature of all, the Presence.

Notably, the Lamb "lights" the city. His presence "powers" it. Revelation clarifies the source of light in the Eternal City.

Revelation 21:11,23-24—

> *It shone with the glory of God, and its brilliance was like that of a very precious jewel, like a jasper, clear as crystal.*

> *The city does not need the sun or the moon to shine on it, **for the glory of God gives it light, and the Lamb is its lamp.** The nations will walk by its light, and the kings of the earth will bring their splendor into it.*

Revelation 22:5—

> *There will be no more night. They will not need the light of a lamp or the light of the sun, for **the Lord God will give them light**. And they will reign for ever and ever.*

It is worth noting also the prophecy of Isaiah 60:19, which is fulfilled by these actions.

Isaiah 60:19—

> *The sun will no more be your light by day, nor will the brightness of the moon shine on you, for **the Lord will be your everlasting light, and your God will be your glory.***

Earlier in our study we mentioned that the Father, the Son, and the Spirit will be present. We want to note that the Father will truly be everywhere in an accessibly greater way than ever before to us. Yet, in a unique way He dwells especially in the New Jerusalem.

Revelation 22:3-5—

> *No longer will there be any curse. **The throne of God and of the Lamb will be in the city, and his servants will serve him. They will see his face**, and his name will be on their foreheads. There will be no more night. They will not need the light of a lamp or the light of the sun, for the Lord God will give them light. And they will reign for ever and ever.*

# 9. Life in Heaven

---

Main idea: Heaven is our permanent home. And, though questions abound, we can take comfort in the fact that God is completely good and He has prepared Heaven with us in mind.

---

*Even though we are living on this earth, Scripture reminds us that "our citizenship is in Heaven, from which also we eagerly wait for a Savior, the Lord Jesus Christ" (Philippians 3:20).*

*If we have but an inkling of what awaits us in the glories of Heaven, we will be like the apostle Paul who eagerly anticipated that future day of resurrection when believers will be conformed to the "body of His glory" (Philippians 3:21).*

*—Paul Enns*[46]

## A. Our permanent, eternal dwelling place

The world where we currently live provides for us something of a foretaste of what we can expect in the world in which we will live compliments of our Heavenly Father and His Son.

Yet, we have become so deeply rooted in this world that it takes a somewhat radical refocus to help us set our affection on Heaven.

---

[46] *Heaven Revealed*, page 184

Colossians 3:1-4—

> *Since, then, you have been raised with Christ,* **set your hearts on things above**, *where Christ is, seated at the right hand of God. Set your minds on things above,* **not on earthly things.** *For you died, and your life is now hidden with Christ in God.*
>
> *When Christ, who is your life, appears, then you also will appear with him in glory.*

Materialism can be a significant distraction that can prove destructive to the Christian life. Unfortunately, what God has provided for us to enjoy in life has become an end in itself. In effect some of the tools and instruments of enjoyment have been allowed to be idols of focus and even obsession.

**Because of our heavenly citizenship we need to cultivate heavenly thinking.** When we reaffix our gaze on heaven and allow ourselves simply to glimpse at earthly enjoyments we become better fitted to prepare ourselves for eternity in a Heavenly country and Heavenly city.

We can look at all things we consider to be bright, beautiful, and even breath-taking and realize that those things and those people are only a glimpse of what God has in store for us and is arranging for us.

Unless we have a focus on Heaven now we cannot correctly interpret and live life on earth. Nothing on earth is permanent in its fallen state. We can learn much about the perspectives our spiritual forefathers adopted.

Hebrews 11 offers us a wealth of wisdom as we pursue the quest to be "heavenly minded."

Hebrews 11:10,13-16—

> *For he was looking forward to the city with foundations, whose architect and builder is God…*

*...All these people were still living by faith when they died. They did not receive the things promised; they only saw them and welcomed them from a distance, admitting that they were foreigners and strangers on earth. People who say such things show that they are looking for a country of their own. If they had been thinking of the country they had left, they would have had opportunity to return.*

*Instead, they were longing for a better country—a heavenly one. Therefore God is not ashamed to be called their God, for he has prepared a city for them.*

One of the best ways to become more "Heavenly minded" is to consider what life will be like when we get there.

## 1. Jesus is preparing a permanent home for us.

Consider the following passages:

John 14:1-6—

*"Do not let your hearts be troubled. You believe in God; believe also in me. My Father's house has many rooms; if that were not so, would I have told you that I am going there to prepare a place for you?* **And if I go and prepare a place for you, I will come back and take you to be with me that you also may be where I am. You know the way to the place where I am going."**

*Thomas said to him, "Lord, we don't know where you are going, so how can we know the way?"*

*Jesus answered, "I am the way and the truth and the life. No one comes to the Father except through me."*

John 17:24—

Father, *I want those you have given me to be with me where I am*, and to see my glory, the glory you have given me because you loved me before the creation of the world.

1 Peter 1:3-5—

*Praise be to the God and Father of our Lord Jesus Christ!*

*In his great mercy he has given us new birth into a living hope through the resurrection of Jesus Christ from the dead, and into an inheritance that can never perish, spoil or fade.*

*This inheritance is kept in heaven for you, who through faith are shielded by God's power until the coming of the salvation that is ready to be revealed in the last time.*

1 John 3:2-3—

*Dear friends, now we are children of God, and what we will be has not yet been made known. But we know that when Christ appears, we shall be like him, for we shall see him as he is. All who have this hope in him purify themselves, just as he is pure.*

2.  **The doctrine of the Resurrection indicates that we will be physical / spiritual beings living in an actual physical universe (as we previously studied).**[47]

The resurrected Christ walked on Earth and occupied space.

Luke 24:39—

*"Look at my hands and my feet. It is I myself! Touch me and see; a ghost does not have flesh and bones, as you see I have."*

---

[47] Review lesson 4.

Even though we are primarily spiritual and not primarily physical, our physical bodies are redeemed. In fact, the entire cosmos is redeemed.

As we read in Alcorn's book[48] *Heaven*—

> *Resurrection does not eliminate space and time, it redeems them.*

> *While God, who is the infinite Creator, inhabits infinity and eternity, man, who is a finite creation, inhabits space and time. Jesus, who is the God-man, inhabits both.*

Many years ago John Newton penned the words to a song appropriate not only for singing but also prayerful meditation, *Amazing Grace*. The entire song contains twelve— yes, a dozen!— verses,

Let's reflect on five of the verses.

> *1 Amazing grace (how sweet the sound)*
> *that saved a wretch like me!*
> *I once was lost, but now am found,*
> *was blind, but now I see.*

> *2 'Twas grace that taught my heart to fear,*
> *and grace my fears relieved;*
> *how precious did that grace appear*
> *the hour I first believed!*

> *3 Through many dangers, toils and snares*
> *I have already come:*
> *'tis grace has brought me safe thus far*
> *and grace will lead me home.*

> *4 The Lord has promised good to me,*

---

[48] *Heaven*, page 266

*his word my hope secures;*
*he will my shield and portion be*
*as long as life endures.*

*5 Yes, when this flesh and heart shall fail,*
*and mortal life shall cease:*
*I shall possess, within the veil,*
*a life of joy and peace.*

# B. Eighteen common questions about Heaven— and our best attempts to answer them

In light of what we've learned about Heaven, let's evaluate some of the most commonly asked questions on the topic.

Before we begin, let's read carefully but without being obsessively analytical some important words from the book of Deuteronomy.

Deuteronomy 29:29—

> *The secret things belong to the Lord our God, but the things revealed belong to us and to our children forever, that we may follow all the words of this law.*

Here are eighteen questions— and best attempts at answers.

1. **Will the New Heaven and New Earth have a sun, a moon, oceans, and weather?**

    Revelation 21:23—

*The city does not need the sun or the moon to shine on it, for the glory of God gives it light, and the Lamb is its lamp.*

Revelation 22:5—

*There will be no more night. They will not need the light of a lamp or the light of the sun, for the Lord God will give them light. And they will reign for ever and ever.*

Isaiah 60:19-21—

*The sun will no more be your light by day, nor will the brightness of the moon shine on you, for the Lord will be your everlasting light, and your God will be your glory.*

*Your sun will never set again, and your moon will wane no more; the Lord will be your everlasting light, and your days of sorrow will end.*

*Then all your people will be righteous and they will possess the land forever. They are the shoot I have planted, the work of my hands, for the display of my splendor.*

Revelation 21:1—

*Then I saw "a new heaven and a new earth," for the first heaven and the first earth had passed away, and there was no longer any sea.*

Isaiah 60:5,9—

*Then you will look and be radiant, your heart will throb and swell with joy; the wealth on the seas will be brought to you, to you the riches of the nations will come…*

*Surely the islands look to me; in the lead are the ships of Tarshish, bringing your children from afar, with their silver and gold, to the honor of the Lord your God, the Holy One of Israel, for he has endowed you with splendor.*

## 2. Will we be ourselves or might we lose ourselves?

You are currently a unique, unrepeatable miracle of God. Individual snowflakes are unique by God's design.

In Heaven you will be what God desires for you to be in terms of personhood, individuality, and identity.

When you are resurrected you certainly will not be *less* of the person you are but truly *more*.

> Luke 15:4-7,10—
>
> *Suppose one of you has a hundred sheep and loses one of them. Doesn't he leave the ninety-nine in the open country and go after the lost sheep until he finds it?*
>
> *And when he finds it, he joyfully puts it on his shoulders and goes home.*
>
> *Then he calls his friends and neighbors together and says, "Rejoice with me; I have found my lost sheep."*
>
> *I tell you that in the same way there will be more rejoicing in heaven over one sinner who repents than over ninety-nine righteous persons who do not need to repent.*
>
> *In the same way, I tell you, there is rejoicing in the presence of the angels of God over one sinner who repents.*

## 3. Will we become angels?

You will not change from being a human being to being an angelic being. Angels are angels, and humans are humans.

Like humans, angels have names, identities, involvements, and histories.

Activities of angels we have heard and read about such as Michael and Gabriel give evidence to these things.

### 4. Will we have emotions and desires?

The Bible tells us that God enjoys, loves, laughs, delights, and rejoices. He is said to also become angry, happy, jealous, glad, and sad.

Since we are partakers of His image and likeness, we are likewise. At times we have "bad" feelings while here on earth.

In Heaven our emotions will be good and edifying.

Revelation 21:4—

*He will wipe every tear from their eyes. There will be no more death or mourning or crying or pain, for the old order of things has passed away.*

Psalm 37:4—

*Take delight in the Lord, and he will give you the desires of your heart.*

### 5. Will we still have our unique personal identities?

Who else could we be except ourselves?

Jesus clearly indicated to the disciples that the resurrected Savior is the same Jesus Christ who died on the Cross.

Luke 24:39—

*"Look at my hands and my feet. It is I myself! Touch me and see; a ghost does not have flesh and bones, as you see I have."*

I will still be me, you will still be you!

## 6. What will our bodies be like?

The Resurrection bodies we receive will be free from the weakness created by the curse of sin. We will be redeemed and restored to the beauty and purpose God intended for us from the foundation of the world.

We will look good with a natural vitality and healthiness not requiring cosmetic disguises and make-up.

## 7. Will we all be extremely beautiful?

The purity and sinlessness from our inner persons with flow into our appearance.

However, we will not compare how good we look to how less than good someone else may look. Our focus will not so much be on our appearance but on our gratitude that we express for our healthiness, vitality, strength, and agility.

## 8. What age will we be?

The debate about our age actually goes in several directions.

Some say age 30, some age 33, some say according to our DNA at our own optimal age, and others opt for a view toward agelessness.

Because our Sovereign Father is our Designer and Creator and Sustainer, I am content to wait expectantly to observe and experience His unfolding plan.

It will be good just as He declared the original to be!

## 9. Will we have our same five senses?

Because our bodies will be similar in fashion to Jesus' resurrected body, we may expect senses like His— at least to a degree. Jesus saw and heard and felt. And, since He cooked fish and ate fish, we surmise that he smelled and tasted it.

Likely our senses will be *more* sensitive and stronger. And it just may be that God may grant us additional senses whereby we can even better perceive and appreciate our environment.

(I am personally looking forward to hearing and seeing better. Regarding my hearing, I feel sure that I am missing a lot of the compliments and expressions of endearment my wife, Joan, is showering upon me.)

## 10. Will we have new abilities?

Our resurrected bodies will not fail us. When Jesus went to Gethsemane with His disciples, they intended to pray while He went into private prayer only to return and find them sleeping.

Matthew 26:41—

> *Watch and pray so that you will not fall into temptation. The spirit is willing, but the flesh is weak.*

While we will not have the same capabilities that Jesus has as the God-Man, we will be like Him and "what we will be has not yet been made known."

1 John 3:2—

> *Dear friends, now we are children of God, and what we will be has not yet been made known. But we know that when Christ appears, we shall be like him, for we shall see him as he is.*

## 11. Will we be male and female?

Some people seek to prove that there will be no gender in Heaven by referring to Paul's statement that in Christ there is neither "male nor female" Galatians 3:28. Paul refers to the reality that already exists on Earth: the equality of men and women in Christ.

Galatians 3:28—

> There is neither Jew nor Gentile, neither slave nor free, nor is there male and female, for you are all one in Christ Jesus.

The issue is not the erasure of sexuality (Adam and Eve had gender before the Fall; you do not surrender your gender when you are converted). Jesus was not gender-neutral after His resurrection.

He was still God-man.

## 12. Will we wear clothes?

In the Present Heaven people appear in white robes depicting righteousness in Christ.

Revelation 3:4—

> Yet you have a few people in Sardis who have not soiled their clothes. They will walk with me, dressed in white, for they are worthy.

Revelation 6:11—

> Then each of them was given a white robe, and they were told to wait a little longer, until the full number of their fellow servants, their brothers and sisters, were killed just as they had been.

Jesus wore clothes after His resurrection.

Clothing in the New Heaven and New Earth may be to enhance appearance and comfort and not for shame or temptation which will not exist.

And our Father Creator will probably provide beautiful apparel based on His instructions for the priests in the Old Testament.

Exodus 28:2—

*Make sacred garments for your brother Aaron to give him dignity and honor.*

Exodus 28:43—

*This is to be a lasting ordinance for Aaron and his descendants.*

## 13. What will we eat and drink— if we eat and drink?

Oddly enough, this is a big topic in Scripture.[49]

*Words describing eating, meals, and food appear over 1,000 times in Scripture, with the English translation 'feast' occurring another 187 times.*

*Feasting involves celebration and fun, and it is profoundly relational…*

*Feasts, including Passover, were spiritual gatherings that drew direct attention to God, His greatness, and His redemptive purposes.*

Some of the Scripture references in and of themselves indicate that eating may be expected in the New Heaven and New Earth.

Some disagree citing the following.

Romans 14:17—

---

[49] Randy Alcorn, *Heaven*, page 301

*For the kingdom of God is not a matter of eating and drinking, but of righteousness, peace and joy in the Holy Spirit.*

Here, however, Paul is reminding believers that the Kingdom is bigger than the feasts of the Old Testament and law-based dietary restrictions— all of which were pointing to the Kingdom itself.

So, consider these passages:

Luke 22:29-30—

*And I confer on you a kingdom, just as my Father conferred one on me, so that you **may eat and drink at my table in my kingdom and sit on thrones**, judging the twelve tribes of Israel.*

Isaiah 25:6—

*On this mountain **the Lord Almighty will prepare a feast** of rich food for all peoples, a banquet of aged wine— the best of meats and the finest of wines.*

John 21:10-15—

*Jesus said to them, "Bring some of the fish you have just caught."*

*So Simon Peter climbed back into the boat and dragged the net ashore. It was full of large fish, 153, but even with so many the net was not torn.*

*Jesus said to them, "Come and have breakfast."*

*None of the disciples dared ask him, "Who are you?" They knew it was the Lord.*

*Jesus came, took the bread and gave it to them, and did the same with the fish.*

*This was now the third time Jesus appeared to his disciples after he was raised from the dead.*

Luke 24:40-43—

*When he had said this, he showed them his hands and feet.*

*And while they still did not believe it because of joy and amazement, he asked them, "Do you have anything here to eat?"*

*They gave him a piece of broiled fish, and he took it and ate it in their presence.*

Acts 10:40-41—

*… but God raised him from the dead on the third day and caused him to be seen.*

*He was not seen by all the people, but by witnesses whom God had already chosen—**by us who ate and drank with him after he rose from the dead**.*

Philippians 3:21—

*… who, by the power that enables him to bring everything under his control, will transform our lowly bodies so that they will be like his glorious body.*

Revelation 19:9—

*Then the angel said to me, "Write this: Blessed are those who are **invited to the wedding supper** of the Lamb!"*

*And he added, "These are the true words of God."*

## 14. Will we get hungry and will we digest food?

Several Scripture references may be prayerfully considered with open and trusting hearts.

Revelation 7:16-17—

> **Never again will they hunger; never again will they thirst.** The sun will not beat down on them, nor any scorching heat.
>
> For the Lamb at the center of the throne will be their shepherd; he will lead them to springs of living water. And God will wipe away every tear from their eyes.

1 Corinthians 6:12-14—

> "I have the right to do anything," you say—but not everything is beneficial.
>
> "I have the right to do anything"—but I will not be mastered by anything.
>
> You say, "Food for the stomach and the stomach for food, and God will destroy them both."
>
> The body, however, is not meant for sexual immorality but for the Lord, and the Lord for the body. By his power God raised the Lord from the dead, and he will raise us also.

Referring to these— and similar— passages, Randy Alcorn makes a helpful observation.[50]

> ...Paul isn't saying that our resurrected bodies won't have stomachs and that we won't eat food on the New Earth...
>
> Could God make it so our new bodies wouldn't go through the same digestive and elimination processes they do now?
>
> Certainly.
>
> Will He?

---

[50] *Heaven*, pages 304-305

*We don't know.*

*But no aspect of our God-created physiology can be bad.*

## 15. Will we be capable of committing sin?

This is a question of great importance. Adam and Eve were also in a sinless environment, but they sinned.

Does our being able to make choices necessitate the ability to choose wrong?

Here is what Scripture promises:

Revelation 21:4—

*He will wipe every tear from their eyes. There will be no more death or mourning or crying or pain, for the old order of things has passed away.*

Romans 6:23—

*For the wages of sin is death, but the gift of God is eternal life in Christ Jesus our Lord.*

With the promise of no more death being a promise of no more sin, Scripture declares clearly that Christ died once to deal with sin and will never need to die again.

Hebrews 9:26-28–

*Otherwise Christ would have had to suffer many times since the creation of the world. But he has appeared once for all at the culmination of the ages to do away with sin by the sacrifice of himself.*

*Just as people are destined to die once, and after that to face judgment, so Christ was sacrificed once to take away the sins of many; and he will appear a second time, not to bear sin, but to bring salvation to those who are waiting for him.*

Hebrews 10:10—

*And by that will, we have been made holy through the sacrifice of the body of Jesus Christ once for all.*

1 Peter 3:18—

*For Christ also suffered once for sins, the righteous for the unrighteous, to bring you to God. He was put to death in the body but made alive in the Spirit.*

## 16. Will we be tempted to sin and if so, will we have free will?

Adam and Eve were innocent but had not received the righteousness purchased by Christ.

Romans 5:19—

*For just as through the disobedience of the one man the many were made sinners, so also **through the obedience of the one man the many will be made righteous.***

God delivers us completely, including vulnerability to sin.

Jesus purchased our perfection forever.

Hebrews 10:14—

*For by one sacrifice **he has made perfect forever those who are being made holy**.*

## 17. Will we be truly perfect?

In *Heaven: A World of Love*, Jonathan Edwards said—

> *Even the very best of men, are, on earth, imperfect. But it is not so in Heaven. There shall be no pollution or deformity or offensive defect of any kind, seen in any person or thing; but every one shall be perfectly pure, and perfectly lovely in heaven.*[51]

Sin is not essential to our humanness. Sin is a defect that has intruded into our humanity because of our wrong choice.

It will be gone.

There will be nothing in Heaven that separates us from God who made us and Who loves us eternally.

## 18. Will we know everything?

**We will certainly know more than we know now, and we will see things much more clearly, but we will never know everything.** God and God alone is omniscient, omnipotent, and omnipresent.

Paul makes a powerful and profound statement.

1 Corinthians 13:12—

> *Now we see but a poor reflection in a mirror; then we shall see face to face. Now I **know** in part; then I shall **know fully**, even as I am **fully known**.*

The words in bold are derived from two different Greek words: *ginosko* and *epiginosko*. The prefix *epi*— intensifies the meaning of *know* resulting in "to really know" or to "know extensively."

---

[51] *Heaven: A World of Love*, Jonathan Edwards. Quoted by Alcorn in *Heaven*, page 314.

**Yet when used of humans it never means absolute knowledge.** We will know in a fuller, more intensive way without any error or misconceptions— not everything. Paul could have used words meaning "all things" if he meant to say "everything." In other words, we will "know fully" yet also receive ongoing, new revelation about the eternal God.

## C. You will fully enjoy Heaven

We've based our answers above on Scripture. However, we're simply taking our "best shot" at understanding an eternal God. **Since God is good, we can affirm Heaven will be everything we've anticipated— and far more**. God fashions us to desire what He will give us, so what God gives us will be exactly what we want.[52]

In part 4 of our study we'll discuss more of what "life in Heaven" will be like. We'll explore our relationships (lesson 10), our ongoing experience (lesson 11), and worship (lesson 12).

---

[52] Randy Alcorn, *Heaven*, page 277

# Part 4 — What Will We Do?

# 10. Destined for Deeper Relationships

---

Main idea: God is relational, and we're created in His image. We were, therefore, designed for relationship—with Him and with others. In Heaven this won't be lessened; it will be amplified.

---

*God has designed us for relationship not only with Himself but also with others of our kind. After God created the world, He stepped back to look at His work and pronounced it "very good."*

*However, before His creation was complete, he said that one thing—and only one—was not good.*

*"It is not good for the man to be alone. I will make a helper suitable for him" (Genesis 2:18).*

*God made people to need and desire others besides Himself.*

*—Randy Alcorn*[53]

---

[53] *Heaven*, page 339

# A. Will we need relationships in addition to our relationship with God in Heaven?

Based on what God Himself said and did for the "first / present earth," **it seems consistent that He would also provide for additional relationships for each of us on the New Heaven and New Earth.**

When we relate to God and His children positively as we will in Heaven, it will not offend God but will please Him— just as it pleases Him now.

There should not be a conflict in our worshipping and relating to God with our primary devotion and attention and also enjoying God's people as well. This would be in accord to the Greatest Commandment.

> Mathew 22:37-39—
>
> *Jesus replied: "'Love the Lord your God with all your heart and with all your soul and with all your mind. **This is the first and greatest commandment. And the second is like it: Love your neighbor as yourself."***

### 1. God's Word is clear that if we love God, we will also love people.

> Luke 10:27-37—
>
> *He answered, "'Love the Lord your God with all your heart and with all your soul and with all your strength and with all your mind and, **Love your neighbor as yourself."***
>
> *"You have answered correctly," Jesus replied. "Do this and you will live."*
>
> *But he wanted to justify himself, so he asked Jesus, "And who is my neighbor?"*

*In reply Jesus said: "A man was going down from Jerusalem to Jericho, when he was attacked by robbers. They stripped him of his clothes, beat him and went away, leaving him half dead.*

*"A priest happened to be going down the same road, and when he saw the man, he passed by on the other side.*

*"So too, a Levite, when he came to the place and saw him, passed by on the other side.*

*"But a Samaritan, as he traveled, came where the man was; and when he saw him, he took pity on him. He went to him and bandaged his wounds, pouring on oil and wine. Then he put the man on his own donkey, brought him to an inn and took care of him. The next day he took out two denarii and gave them to the innkeeper. 'Look after him,' he said, 'and when I return, I will reimburse you for any extra expense you may have.'*

*"Which of these three do you think was a neighbor to the man who fell into the hands of robbers?"*

*The expert in the law replied, **"The one who had mercy on him."***

*Jesus told him, "Go and do likewise."*

1 John 4:7-12—

*Dear friends, **let us love one another, for love comes from God.** Everyone who loves has been born of God and knows God.*

*Whoever does not love does not know God, because God is love.*

*This is how God showed his love among us: He sent his one and only Son into the world that we might live through him.*

*This is love: not that we loved God, but that he loved us and sent his Son as an atoning sacrifice for our sins.*

> *Dear friends,* **since God so loved us, we also ought to love one another.**
>
> *No one has ever seen God; but* **if we love one another, God lives in us and his love is made complete in us.**

2.  **Heaven will not eradicate the ways in which we express love. Rather, Heaven will enhance how we love.**

    For the remainder of this lesson we will evaluate the following:

    **B. How we will relate to ourselves**

    **C. How we will relate to others**

    **D. How we will relate to God**

# B. How we will relate to ourselves

1.  **We will retain our identities and personalities.**

    Some have wondered if being like Jesus (1 John 3:2) means that we will lose self-identity.

    1 John 3:2—

    > *Dear friends, now we are children of God, and what we will be has not yet been made known. But we know that when Christ appears, we shall be like him, for we shall see him as he is.*

    Randy Alcorn answers,

*We can all be like Jesus in character yet remain very different from one another in personality.*[54]

He continues,

*We will be real people with real desires, but our desires will be holy desires. We will have real feelings, but our feelings will be redeemed from pride, insecurity, and wrong thinking.* **We will be ourselves but with all the good and none of the bad.**[55]

Notice the following pages, which seem to indicate we will remain "who we are" in Heaven.

Job 19:26-27—

*And after my skin has been destroyed,* **yet in my flesh I will see God; I myself will see him with my own eyes—I, and not another.** *How my heart yearns within me!*

Matthew 17:1-4—

*After six days Jesus took with him Peter, James, and John the brother of James, and led them up a high mountain by themselves. There* **he was transfigured before them.** *His face shone like the sun, and his clothes became as white as the light.* **Just then there appeared before them Moses and Elijah, talking with Jesus.**

*Peter said to Jesus, "Lord, it is good for us to be here. If you wish, I will put up three shelters—one for you, one for Moses, and one for Elijah."*

Luke 24:39—

---

[54] Randy Alcorn, *50 Days…*, page174

[55] Randy Alcorn, *50 Days…*, page 174

*"Look at my hands and my feet. **It is I myself! Touch me and see;** a ghost does not have flesh and bones, as you see I have."*

John 20:28—

*Thomas said to him, "My Lord and my God!"*

John 21:7—

*Then the disciple whom Jesus loved said to Peter, "**It is the Lord!**"*

*As soon as Simon Peter heard him say, "It is the Lord," he wrapped his outer garment around him (for he had taken it off) and jumped into the water.*

As we have said, we will change— we will be "upgraded." But, we will still be who we are.

1 Corinthians 15:42-44—

*So will it be with the resurrection of the dead. The body that is sown is perishable, it is raised imperishable; it is sown in dishonor, it is raised in glory; it is sown in weakness, it is raised in power; it is sown a natural body, it is raised a spiritual body.*

*If there is a natural body, there is also a spiritual body.*

2.  **We will be given a "new name."**

When Revelation 20:15 and 21:27 speaks of the Lamb's Book of Life and the names of God's children written therein, those names seem to be our earthly names.

Revelation 20:15—

*Anyone whose name was not found written in the book of life was thrown into the lake of fire.*

Revelation 21:27—

> *Nothing impure will ever enter it, nor will anyone who does what is shameful or deceitful, but only those whose names are written in the Lamb's book of life.*

Since our names indicate our individuality and God calls people by their earthly names – Abraham, Isaac, Jacob. Our names speak of continuity between life now and the future.

**Even so we will receive new names in Heaven as noted in various passages.**

Isaiah 62:2—

> *The nations will see your vindication, and all kings your glory;* ***you will be called by a new name*** *that the mouth of the Lord will bestow.*

Isaiah 65:15—

> *You will leave your name for my chosen ones to use in their curses; the Sovereign Lord will put you to death, but* ***to his servants he will give another name.***

Revelation 2:17,3:12—

> *Whoever has ears, let them hear what the Spirit says to the churches. To the one who is victorious, I will give some of the hidden manna.* ***I will also give that person a white stone with a new name written on it****, known only to the one who receives it…*

> *The one who is victorious I will make a pillar in the temple of my God. Never again will they leave it. I will write on them the name of my God and the name of the city of my God, the new Jerusalem, which is coming down out of heaven from my God; and* ***I will also write on them my new name.***

### 3. We will retain our ethnic identities.

The New Jerusalem will be a melting pot of diversity, reflecting the intent and accomplishment of the Commission of Jesus our Lord in Matthew 28:18-20. He declared His expectation to His disciples following His resurrection, at the time of His ascension.

Matthew 28:18-20—

> Then Jesus came to them and said, "All authority in heaven and on earth has been given to me. Therefore go and make **disciples of all nations**, baptizing them in the name of the Father and of the Son and of the Holy Spirit, and teaching them to obey everything I have commanded you. And surely I am with you always, to the very end of the age."

Our diversity will be celebrated as noted in Revelation 5:9-10.

Revelation 5:9-10—

> And they sang a new song, saying: "You are worthy to take the scroll and to open its seals, because you were slain, and with your blood you purchased for God **persons from every tribe and language and people and nation. You have made them to be a kingdom and priests** to serve our God, and they will reign on the earth."

The division of Jews and Gentiles will have been completely resolved according to Ephesians 2:14-16.

Ephesians 2:14-16—

> For he himself is our peace, who has made the two groups one and has destroyed the barrier, the dividing wall of hostility, by setting aside in his flesh the law with its commands and regulations. **His purpose was to create in himself one new humanity out of the two, thus making peace**, and in one body to reconcile both of them to God through the cross, by which he put to death their hostility.

**While there will be one new humanity, we will still retain our unique diversity.** Daniel expressed that the Messiah would be given unique rulership— and create unparalleled unity— among diverse groups.

Daniel 7:14—

He was given authority, glory and sovereign power; **all nations and peoples of every language worshiped him**. His dominion is an everlasting dominion that will not pass away, and his kingdom is one that will never be destroyed.

4. **We will have perfect bodies— without faults or infirmities.**

Notice what the Bible tells us.

1 Corinthians 15:35-54—

But someone will ask, "How are the dead raised? With what kind of body will they come?"

How foolish! What you sow does not come to life unless it dies. When you sow, you do not plant the body that will be, but just a seed, perhaps of wheat or of something else. But God gives it a body as he has determined, and to each kind of seed he gives its own body.

Not all flesh is the same: People have one kind of flesh, animals have another, birds another and fish another. There are also heavenly bodies and there are earthly bodies; but the splendor of the heavenly bodies is one kind, and the splendor of the earthly bodies is another. The sun has one kind of splendor, the moon another and the stars another; and star differs from star in splendor.

So will it be with the resurrection of the dead. **The body that is sown is perishable, it is raised imperishable; it is sown in**

**dishonor, it is raised in glory; it is sown in weakness, it is raised in power; it is sown a natural body, it is raised a spiritual body.**

*If there is a natural body, there is also a spiritual body. So it is written: "The first man Adam became a living being"; the last Adam, a life-giving spirit.*

*The spiritual did not come first, but the natural, and after that the spiritual. The first man was of the dust of the earth; the second man is of heaven. As was the earthly man, so are those who are of the earth; and as is the heavenly man, so also are those who are of heaven. And just as we have borne the image of the earthly man, so shall we bear the image of the heavenly man.*

*I declare to you, brothers and sisters, that flesh and blood cannot inherit the kingdom of God, nor does the perishable inherit the imperishable.*

*Listen, I tell you a mystery: We will not all sleep, but we will all be changed— in a flash, in the twinkling of an eye, at the last trumpet. For the trumpet will sound, the dead will be raised imperishable, and we will be changed.*

***For the perishable must clothe itself with the imperishable, and the mortal with immortality***. *When the perishable has been clothed with the imperishable, and the mortal with immortality, then the saying that is written will come true: "Death has been swallowed up in victory."*

Robert Jeffress insightfully describes the benefit of our resurrected bodies and our increased knowledge:

*Our earthly bodies decay; our Heavenly bodies endure. Our earthly bodies are infected with sin; our Heavenly bodies will be free of sin. Our earthly bodies are weak; our Heavenly bodies will be powerful. Our earthly bodies are for the Old Earth; our Heavenly bodies will be for the New Heaven and Earth.*[56]

5. **We will not remember things which bring sorrow or sadness... or, at least, we will understand them in a new way.**

Our memories will be improved in Heaven not lessened. The reality of the principle of continuity indicates that we will remember our past.

Yet, in Heaven because we are forgiven with the erasing of our sin, we will still be able to recall what we need to recall to remind us of the power and magnitude of God's mercy, grace, and love.

Isaiah 65:19—

*I will rejoice over Jerusalem and take delight in my people; **the sound of weeping and of crying will be heard in it no more**.*

Philippians 3:12-14—

*Not that I have already obtained all this, or have already arrived at my goal, but I press on to take hold of that for which Christ Jesus took hold of me.*

*Brothers and sisters, I do not consider myself yet to have taken hold of it. But one thing I do: **Forgetting what is behind and straining toward what is ahead, I press on toward the goal to win the prize** for which God has called me heavenward in Christ Jesus.*

Evidently we will have the capacity to choose to recall or to choose not to recall the things that might hinder us from experiencing the joy of Heaven. God, who is omniscient, told Jeremiah that, in regard to Israel, He is able to "forget."

---

[56] See his book, *A Place Called Heaven,* pages158-168.

Jeremiah 31:34—

> "No longer will they teach their neighbor, or say to one another, 'Know the Lord,' because they will all know me, from the least of them to the greatest," declares the Lord. "**For I will forgive their wickedness and will remember their sins no more.**"

What about loved ones, friends, and family who are not with us in Heaven?

Will they be forgotten?

Will we grieve over them?

Revelation 21:3-5—

> And I heard a loud voice from the throne saying, "Look! God's dwelling place is now among the people, and he will dwell with them. **They will be his people, and God himself will be with them and be their God. He will wipe every tear from their eyes. There will be no more death or mourning or crying or pain, for the old order of things has passed away.**"
>
> He who was seated on the throne said, "I am making everything new!" Then he said, "Write this down, for these words are trustworthy and true."

# C. How we will relate to others

As we've seen, love of God always overflows and expresses itself through the tangible ways we love others. This will be true even in— *especially* in— Heaven. Here are five observations about relationships with others in Heaven.

## 1. We will be reunited with our families and friends.

A significant number of Scriptures clearly indicate that there will be reunion with our loved ones.

1 Thessalonians 2:8,17,19-20—

> *...so we cared for you. Because we loved you so much, we were delighted to share with you not only the gospel of God but our lives as well...*
>
> *But, brothers and sisters, when we were orphaned by being separated from you for a short time (in person, not in thought), out of our intense longing we made every effort to see you.*
>
> ***For what is our hope, our joy, or the crown in which we will glory in the presence of our Lord Jesus when he comes? Is it not you?***
>
> *Indeed, you are our glory and joy.*

1 Thessalonians 3:6-10—

> *But Timothy has just now come to us from you and has brought good news about your faith and love. He has told us that you always have pleasant memories of us and that you long to see us, **just as we also long to see you.***
>
> *Therefore, brothers and sisters, in all our distress and persecution we were encouraged about you because of your faith. For now we really live, since you are standing firm in the Lord.*
>
> ***How can we thank God enough for you in return for all the joy we have in the presence of our God because of you?***
>
> *Night and day we pray most earnestly that we may see you again and supply what is lacking in your faith.*

1 Thessalonians 4:13-14,17-18—

*Brothers and sisters, we do not want you to be uninformed about those who sleep in death, so that you do not grieve like the rest of mankind, who have no hope. For we believe that Jesus died and rose again, and **so we believe that God will bring with Jesus those who have fallen asleep in him.***

*According to the Lord's word, we tell you that we who are still alive, who are left until the coming of the Lord, will certainly not precede those who have fallen asleep. For the Lord himself will come down from heaven, with a loud command, with the voice of the archangel, and with the trumpet call of God, and the dead in Christ will rise first.*

*After that, **we who are still alive and are left will be caught up together with them in the clouds to meet the Lord in the air. And so we will be with the Lord forever.***

*Therefore encourage one another with these words.*

When reading the Epistles of Paul, we cannot miss the Apostle's affection for his friends and brothers and sisters in Christ. This affection led Paul also to his expression to some of them of his expectation of a future with them in Heaven.

Especially helpful, as well, are the words about Abraham, Isaac, and Jacob throughout Genesis.

Genesis 25:8 (referring to Abraham)–

*Then Abraham breathed his last and died at a good old age, an old man and full of years; and **he was gathered to his people.***

Genesis 35:29 (about Isaac)–

*Then he breathed his last and died and **was gathered to his people**, old and full of years. And his sons Esau and Jacob buried him.*

Genesis 49:33 (about Jacob)—

> *When Jacob had finished giving instructions to his sons, he drew his feet up into the bed, **breathed his last and was gathered to his people.***

In addition when David's infant son from Bathsheba died he was confident that he would be reunited with him in Heaven. He expressed it clearly.

2 Samuel 12:23—

> *But now that he is dead, why should I go on fasting? Can I bring him back again? **I will go to him, but he will not return to me.***

2. **We will know each other even better and more completely.**

We will experience the ability to relate to each other without the barriers that are a part of our humanity at the current time. Our knowledge will not be limited to the hindrances that keep us from the deeper relationships which we truly desire.

A significant factor that makes possible this knowledge involves our resurrection bodies and their similarity to Jesus' resurrection body.

Notice the following passages.

John 21:1-14—

> *Afterward Jesus appeared again to his disciples, by the Sea of Galilee. It happened this way: Simon Peter, Thomas (also known as Didymus), Nathanael from Cana in Galilee, the sons of Zebedee, and two other disciples were together.*
>
> *"I'm going out to fish," Simon Peter told them, and they said, "We'll go with you."*
>
> *So they went out and got into the boat, but that night they caught nothing.*

*Early in the morning, Jesus stood on the shore, but the disciples did not realize that it was Jesus.*

*He called out to them, "Friends, haven't you any fish?"*

*"No," they answered.*

*He said, "Throw your net on the right side of the boat and you will find some." When they did, they were unable to haul the net in because of the large number of fish.*

*Then the disciple whom Jesus loved said to Peter, "**It is the Lord!**"*

*As soon as Simon Peter heard him say, "It is the Lord," he wrapped his outer garment around him (for he had taken it off) and jumped into the water.*

*The other disciples followed in the boat, towing the net full of fish, for they were not far from shore, about a hundred yards.*

*When they landed, they saw a fire of burning coals there with fish on it, and some bread.*

*Jesus said to them, "Bring some of the fish you have just caught."*

*So Simon Peter climbed back into the boat and dragged the net ashore. It was full of large fish, 153, but even with so many the net was not torn.*

*Jesus said to them, "Come and have breakfast."*

***None of the disciples dared ask him, "Who are you?"***

***They knew it was the Lord.***

*Jesus came, took the bread and gave it to them, and did the same with the fish.*

*This was now the third time Jesus appeared to his disciples after he was raised from the dead.*

1 Corinthians 13:9-12—

> *For we know in part and we prophesy in part, but when completeness comes, **what is in part disappears**.*
>
> *When I was a child, I talked like a child, I thought like a child, I reasoned like a child. When I became a man, I put the ways of childhood behind me.*
>
> *For now we see only a reflection as in a mirror; then we shall see face to face. **Now I know in part; then I shall know fully, even as I am fully known.***

Because we are able to see "fully" instead of with a limited perspective, our relationships will become deeper— in every direction. We will know each other fully.

Notice the following:

Isaiah 65:16-19—

> *Whoever invokes a blessing in the land will do so by the one true God; whoever takes an oath in the land will swear by the one true God. For the past troubles will be forgotten and hidden from my eyes.*
>
> *See, I will create new heavens and a new earth. The former things will not be remembered, nor will they come to mind.*
>
> *But be glad and rejoice forever in what I will create, for I will create Jerusalem to be a delight and its people a joy.*
>
> ***I will rejoice over Jerusalem and take delight in my people; the sound of weeping and of crying will be heard in it no more.***

John 20:24-29—

> *Now Thomas (also known as Didymus), one of the Twelve, was not with the disciples when Jesus came.*

*So the other disciples told him, "We have seen the Lord!"*

*But he said to them, "Unless I see the nail marks in his hands and put my finger where the nails were, and put my hand into his side, I will not believe."*

*A week later his disciples were in the house again, and Thomas was with them.*

*Though the doors were locked, Jesus came and stood among them and said, "Peace be with you!"*

*Then he said to Thomas, "Put your finger here; see my hands. Reach out your hand and put it into my side. Stop doubting and believe."*

***Thomas said to him, "My Lord and my God!"***

*Then Jesus told him, "Because you have seen me, you have believed; blessed are those who have not seen and yet have believed."*

Philippians 1:3-8—

*I thank my God every time I remember you. In all my prayers for all of you, I always pray with joy because of your partnership in the gospel from the first day until now, being confident of this, that **he who began a good work in you will carry it on to completion until the day of Christ Jesus.***

*It is right for me to feel this way about all of you, since I have you in my heart and, whether I am in chains or defending and confirming the gospel, all of you share in God's grace with me. God can testify how I long for all of you with the affection of Christ Jesus.*

Philippians 1:21-24—

*For to me, to live is Christ and to die is gain. If I am to go on living in the body, this will mean fruitful labor for me. Yet what shall I choose? I do not know! I am torn between the two: I desire to depart and be with Christ, which is better by far; but it is more necessary for you that I remain in the body.*

3. **We will love each other more deeply, in a greater dimension—and, as result, experience true community /** *koinonia***.**

Our devotion to God bonds us more closely to fellow believers than even our biological family ties. Even so, **our love for family and friends in Christ will move to a deeper level in Heaven**.

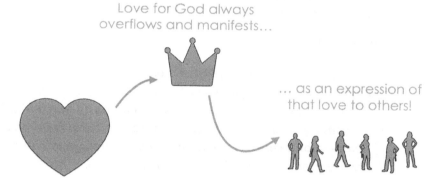

Love for God always overflows and manifests...

... as an expression of that love to others!

*EVEN IN HEAVEN— ESPECIALLY IN HEAVEN!*

John 13:33-36—

*"My children, I will be with you only a little longer. You will look for me, and just as I told the Jews, so I tell you now: Where I am going, you cannot come.*

*"A new command I give you: Love one another. As I have loved you, so you must love one another.* **By this everyone will know that you are my disciples, if you love one another.***"*

*Simon Peter asked him, "Lord, where are you going?"*

*Jesus replied, "Where I am going, you cannot follow now, but you will follow later."*

Luke 8:19-21—

*Now Jesus' mother and brothers came to see him, but they were not able to get near him because of the crowd.*

*Someone told him, "Your mother and brothers are standing outside, wanting to see you."*

*He replied,* **"My mother and brothers are those who hear God's word and put it into practice.***"*

Mark 10:29-31—

*"Truly I tell you," Jesus replied, "no one who has left home or brothers or sisters or mother or father or children or fields for me and the gospel will fail to* **receive a hundred times as much in this present age: homes, brothers, sisters, mothers, children and fields—along with persecutions—and in the age to come eternal life***. But many who are first will be last, and the last first."*

We will enjoy this deeper, true fellowship, because we are created in God's image. And, God is relational.

Genesis 1:26—

*Then God said,* **"Let us** *make mankind in our image, in our likeness, so that they may rule over the fish in the sea and the birds in the sky, over the livestock and all the wild animals, and over all the creatures that move along the ground."*

Luke 10:21-23—

> At that time Jesus, full of joy through the Holy Spirit, said, "I praise you, Father, Lord of heaven and earth, because you have hidden these things from the wise and learned, and revealed them to little children. Yes, Father, for this is what you were pleased to do.
>
> **"All things have been committed to me by my Father. No one knows who the Son is except the Father, and no one knows who the Father is except the Son and those to whom the Son chooses to reveal him."**
>
> Then he turned to his disciples and said privately, "Blessed are the eyes that see what you see…"

Matthew 8:11—

> I say to you that many will come from the east and the west, and will **take their places at the feast with Abraham, Isaac and Jacob in the kingdom of heaven**.

Randy Alcorn in his shorter book about Heaven, *50 Days of Heaven*, expresses the relational dynamics of Heaven well:

> In Heaven, there won't be cliques, exclusion, arrogance, posturing, belittling help, or jealousy. When friends particularly enjoy each other's company, that's as God designed it.[57]

He goes on to remind us that we will experience the joy of familiarity in old relationships and the joy of discovery in new relationships.

The *koinonia* that the early New Testament church experienced in Acts 2 will be renewed and established in total fullness in the New Heaven and the New Earth.

---

[57] Randy Alcorn, *50 Days of Heaven*, page 210.

# KOINONIA

Greek, the language of the New Testament

19 specific appearances in Scripture

COMMUNITY

COMMUNION

JOINT PARTICIPATION

SHARING

INTIMACY

ONENESS

FULL ACCEPTANCE

We will not be concerned about deception or ulterior motives of those with whom we fellowship or converse. The entire environment will be saturated with love, joy, peace, long-suffering, gentleness, goodness, faith, meekness, and self-control. In other words, the fruit of the Holy Spirit will flow forth from every person without exception.

4. **Marriage will (likely) change, yet we must remember that God always "trades up" in His plan of redemption.**

Will marriage exist in Heaven?

Notice what Paul says in his teaching about marriage.

Ephesians 5:25-32—

*Husbands, love your wives, just as Christ loved the church and gave himself up for her to make her holy, cleansing her by the washing with water through the word, and to present her to himself as a radiant church, without stain or wrinkle or any other blemish, but holy and blameless.*

*In this same way, husbands ought to love their wives as their own bodies. He who loves his wife loves himself. After all, no one ever hated their own body, but they feed and care for their body, just as Christ does the church— for we are members of his body.*

*"For this reason a man will leave his father and mother and be united to his wife, and the two will become one flesh."*

**This is a profound mystery—but I am talking about Christ and the church.**

Notice the "odd" nature of this passage. Even though we initially think Paul is talking about marriage between a man and a woman, he purports to write about Christ and His bride, the Church.

Jesus spoke of marriage in Heaven in a confrontation with the Pharisees. It's important to remember, though, that the Pharisees were not looking for an actual answer. Rather, they were trying to "trap" Jesus by getting Him to answer a hypothetical question in the wrong way to trap Him.

Matthew 22:28-30—

*Now then, at the resurrection, whose wife will she be of the seven, since all of them were married to her?"*

*Jesus replied, "You are in error because you do not know the Scriptures or the power of God. At the resurrection people will neither marry nor be given in marriage; they will be like the angels in heaven."*

Regardless of their motivation in questioning Him, we can stand assured that Jesus spoke truth.

So, will we be married in Heaven? Will there by marriage?

Yes and no.

The Scripture makes it clear that there will be marriage in Heaven.

**What the Bible clearly says is that there will be one marriage which is to be between Christ and His Bride, the Church.**

Again, Paul makes it clear in Ephesians 5:25-30 that **the union we know now as marriage is a signpost indicating that our relationship on earth points us to our relationship with Christ to His Bride**. The signpost (earthly marriage, which points to the Heavenly encounter) will not be necessary on the New Heaven and New Earth.

At the same time, **based on other truths we have learned, we can affirm that we will not become distant from our best friends in Heaven.** That means that even though we are no longer married to each other in the sense that we were on earth, God will in all likelihood enhance our relationship with those with whom we have experienced the joys and fulfillment of marriage.

Remember, in Heaven things are better— not "less." This is true even if we don't yet understand the full ramifications of what life will be like when we get there.

At the time of this writing, my precious wife, Joan, and I have been married for 53, soon to be 54 years. I completely expect to be closer to Joan than I am now. I am grateful to God, our Father, for the remarkable relationship we have had for more than five decades.

(It should be quickly added that I sincerely mean it when I testify that the Lord God and Joan are to be applauded and credited with the remarkable miracle our marriage has been. In fact, Joan and I collaborated and developed a series of marital seminars entitled The Miracle of Marriage, available at no charge on our website.)

I believe our friendship will be even richer in Heaven.

This leads to a follow-up question…

5. **Will sexuality exist in Heaven?**

And what about the intimacy and fulfillment of sexual relations?

Since God is changing and fulfilling a part of His eternal plan, it seems to me and to others, I feel sure that He would not take away something so wonderful without providing something just as wonderful and probably more so.

C.S. Lewis referred to sexuality in Heaven and noted—

> I think our present outlook might be like that of a small boy who, on being told that the sexual act was the highest bodily pleasure, should immediately ask whether you ate chocolates at the same time..
>
> On receiving the answer "No," he might regard absence of chocolates as the chief characteristic of sexuality. In vain would you tell him that the reason why lovers in their carnal raptures don't bother about chocolates is that they have something better to think of.
>
> The boy knows chocolate: he does not know the positive thing that excludes it.
>
> We are in the same position. We know the sexual life; we do not know, except in glimpses, the other thing which, in Heaven, will leave no room for it.[58]

Again, while we currently live on earth (first earth), our future is on the New Heaven and New Earth. Whatever is good and satisfying here on earth will be improved upon in Heaven.  Fallen earth will be renewed and renovated and the curse of the Fall of man and the universe will be removed. Heaven is always better than earth.

Several years ago I listened intently to a message delivered by long-time pastor and teacher, Charles Carter.[59] He told of a time when another pastor-friend took his own son— who was at that time just a young boy— to hear a

---

[58] Quoted by Randy Alcorn, *Heaven*, page 354.

[59] Charles Carter served at Shades Mountain Baptist Church in Birmingham, Alabama.

testimony shared by Tim Tebow, the Heisman Trophy winning football player for the University of Florida.

As they were leaving, Charles Carter's friend asked his son what he thought about the message and challenge delivered by Tebow.

His son responded readily: "Well, Dad, let me ask you. I would have no problem giving up drugs or drinking alcohol. But, I don't think I can give up pre-meal snacks."

(Did he mean "pre-meal snacks" or did he mis-hear premarital sex?!)

Sexuality is woven into our lives currently by God Himself. As a good, good Father who has always provided quite all and everything we need, He will continue to fulfill every appropriate need and desire that we have on the New Heaven and New Earth.

Paul Enns clarifies this perspective:

> There is no realm in which Earth is better. In no way will we ever be poorer in Heaven than on earth.[60]

# D. How we will relate to God

In Heaven, we will finally experience fullness of relationship with God.

Remember what Jesus prayed in the Upper Room as He approached His betrayal.

Jesus defined "eternal life" as "knowing God."[61]

John 17:3—

---

[60] See his book *Heaven Revealed*, pages 157-171.

[61] We evaluated this point for a full lesson in chapter 3.

**Now this is eternal life: that they know you, the only true God, and Jesus Christ, whom you have sent.**

This theme continues throughout the entire chapter of John 17.

John 17—

*After Jesus said this, he looked toward heaven and prayed:*

*"Father, the hour has come. Glorify your Son, that your Son may glorify you. For you granted him authority over all people that he might give eternal life to all those you have given him.*

*"**Now this is eternal life: that they know you, the only true God, and Jesus Christ, whom you have sent.** I have brought you glory on earth by finishing the work you gave me to do. And now, Father, glorify me in your presence with the glory I had with you before the world began.*

*"I have revealed you to those whom you gave me out of the world. They were yours; you gave them to me and they have obeyed your word. Now they know that everything you have given me comes from you.*

*"For I gave them the words you gave me and they accepted them. They knew with certainty that I came from you, and they believed that you sent me.*

*"I pray for them. I am not praying for the world, but for those you have given me, for they are yours. All I have is yours, and all you have is mine. And glory has come to me through them. I will remain in the world no longer, but they are still in the world, and I am coming to you.*

*"Holy Father, protect them by the power of your name, the name you gave me, so that they may be one as we are one. While I was with them, I protected them and kept them safe by that name you gave me. None has been lost except the one doomed to destruction so that Scripture would be fulfilled.*

*"I am coming to you now, but I say these things while I am still in the world, **so that they may have the full measure of my joy within them**. I have*

*given them your word and the world has hated them, for they are not of the world any more than I am of the world.*

*"My prayer is not that you take them out of the world but that you protect them from the evil one. They are not of the world, even as I am not of it. Sanctify them by the truth; your word is truth. As you sent me into the world, I have sent them into the world. For them I sanctify myself, that they too may be truly sanctified.*

*"My prayer is not for them alone. I pray also for those who will believe in me through their message, that all of them may be one, Father, **just as you are in me and I am in you. May they also be in us** so that the world may believe that you have sent me. I have given them the glory that you gave me, that they may be one as we are one— **I in them and you in me—so that they may be brought to complete unity.** Then the world will know that you sent me and have loved them even as you have loved me.*

*"Father, I want those you have given me to be with me where I am, and to see my glory, the glory you have given me because you loved me before the creation of the world.*

*"Righteous Father, though the world does not know you, I know you, and they know that you have sent me. I have made you known to them, and will continue to make you known in order that the love you have for me may be in them and that I myself may be in them."*

Here are four facts about our relationship with God in Heaven.

## 1.  We will see Him— and we will know Him.[62]

Remember how God related to Israel.

Exodus 19:16—

---

[62] See Paul Enns, *Heaven Revealed*, pages 173-182.

*On the morning of the third day there was thunder and lightning, with a thick cloud over the mountain, and a very loud trumpet blast. Everyone in the camp trembled.*

Exodus 33:20—

*"But," he said, "**you cannot see my face, for no one may see me and live.**"*

Eventually, people did see God— and survived. But, not without much overwhelm and anxiety.

Isaiah 6:5—

*"Woe to me!" I cried. "**I am ruined!** For I am a man of unclean lips, and I live among a people of unclean lips, and **my eyes have seen the King, the Lord Almighty.**"*

Job declared one day he would see God. In fact, he longed too.

Job 19:26-27—

*And after my skin has been destroyed, yet in my flesh **I will see God; I myself will see him with my own eyes**—I, and not another. How my heart yearns within me!*

Of course, Jesus promised that the pure in heart would— will— see God.

Matthew 5:8—

*Blessed are the pure in heart, for **they will see God.**

Seeing God and knowing God is beyond comprehension on the present earth. But, we will see Him in the future.

1 John 3:2—

*Dear friends, now we are children of God, and what we will be has not yet been made known. But **we know that when Christ appears, we shall be like him, for we shall see him as he is.***

One of the most profound statements in Scripture. "We shall see Him just as He is." This leads us to our next observation— also mentioned in 1 John 3:2.

## 2.  We will also be like Him.

This will be the last stage of our complete redemption and salvation.

1 Thessalonians 4:16-17—

*For the Lord himself will come down from heaven, with a loud command, with the voice of the archangel, and with the trumpet call of God, and the dead in Christ will rise first. After that, we who are still alive and are left will be caught up together with them in the clouds to **meet the Lord in the air. And so we will be with the Lord forever.***

1 Corinthians 15:52-53—

*… in a flash, in the twinkling of an eye, at the last trumpet. For the trumpet will sound, the dead will be raised imperishable, and **we will be changed.***

*For the perishable must **clothe itself with the imperishable, and the mortal with immortality.***

On the great resurrection day we will receive imperishable, sinless, glorified bodies— in that sense be like Him.

## 3.  We will have close association with Jesus the Son and with God the Father.

The actual "Lord's Prayer" (John 17, quoted earlier in this section of the chapter, as opposed to the "Model Prayer" in Matthew 6:9-13 and Luke 11:2-4) was offered by Jesus to the Father in the last hours before His trials and crucifixion.

Notice a portion of that prayer all of which is so filled with meaning…

John 17:24-26—

*Father, **I want those you have given me to be with me where I am, and to see my glory**, the glory you have given me because you loved me before the creation of the world.*

*Righteous Father, though the world does not know you, I know you, and they know that you have sent me. I have made you known to them, and **will continue to make you known in order that the love you have for me may be in them and that I myself may be in them**.*

The Scripture declares we will live in close proximity to God.

Revelation 21:3—

*And I heard a loud voice from the throne saying, "Look! **God's dwelling place is now among the people**, and he will dwell with them. They will be his people, and **God himself will be with them and be their God**."*

This leads to our final observation about our connection to God in Heaven.

## 4. We will worship and marvel.

In that day, we will not argue over the style of music. There will be total unity and harmony in worship. We will be so focused on pure spiritual worship of the Triune God that there will be no time or place for personal preference. We will focus on glorifying the Worthy One.

Isaiah 66:22-23—

*"As the new heavens and the new earth that I make will endure before me," declares the Lord, "so will your name and descendants endure. From one New Moon to another and from one Sabbath to another, **all mankind will come and bow down before me,**" says the Lord.*

Revelation 4:1-11—

*After this I looked, and there before me was a door standing open in heaven.*

*And the voice I had first heard speaking to me like a trumpet said, "Come up here, and I will show you what must take place after this."*

*At once I was in the Spirit, and there before me was a throne in heaven with someone sitting on it. And the one who sat there had the appearance of jasper and ruby. A rainbow that shone like an emerald encircled the throne.*

*Surrounding the throne were twenty-four other thrones, and seated on them were twenty-four elders. They were dressed in white and had crowns of gold on their heads. From the throne came flashes of lightning, rumblings and peals of thunder.*

*In front of the throne, seven lamps were blazing. These are the seven spirits of God. Also in front of the throne there was what looked like a sea of glass, clear as crystal.*

*In the center, around the throne, were four living creatures, and they were covered with eyes, in front and in back. The first living creature was like a lion, the second was like an ox, the third had a face like a man, the fourth was like a flying eagle. Each of the four living creatures had six wings and was covered with eyes all around, even under its wings.*

***Day and night they never stop saying: "Holy, holy, holy is the Lord God Almighty, who was, and is, and is to come."***

*Whenever the living creatures give glory, honor and thanks to him who sits on the throne and who lives for ever and ever, the twenty-four elders fall down before him who sits on the throne and worship him who lives for ever and ever.*

***They lay their crowns before the throne*** *and say, "You are worthy, our Lord and God, to receive glory and honor and power, for you created all things, and by your will they were created and have their being."*

Revelation 5:9-14—

*And they sang a new song, saying: "You are worthy to take the scroll and to open its seals, because you were slain, and with your blood you purchased for God persons from every tribe and language and people and nation. You have made them to be a kingdom and priests to serve our God, and they will reign on the earth."*

*Then I looked and heard **the voice of many angels, numbering thousands upon thousands, and ten thousand times ten thousand.** They encircled the throne and the living creatures and the elders.*

*In a loud voice they were saying: "Worthy is the Lamb, who was slain, to receive power and wealth and wisdom and strength and honor and glory and praise!"*

***Then I heard every creature in heaven and on earth and under the earth and on the sea, and all that is in them, saying: "To him who sits on the throne and to the Lamb be praise and honor and glory and power, for ever and ever!"***

*The four living creatures said, "Amen," and the elders fell down and worshiped.*

Revelation 21:22-27—

*I did not see a temple in the city, because the Lord God Almighty and the Lamb are its temple. The city does not need the sun or the moon to shine on it, for the glory of God gives it light, and the Lamb is its lamp. The nations will walk by its light, and the kings of the earth will bring their splendor into it.*

*On no day will its gates ever be shut, for there will be no night there.*

***The glory and honor of the nations will be brought into it.***
*Nothing impure will ever enter it, nor will anyone who does what is shameful or deceitful, but only those whose names are written in the Lamb's book of life.*

One of the wonderful local churches where I was privileged to pastor purchased property for an expected time of relocation as the church grew. Calvary Baptist Church in Rosenberg, Texas grew and felt the time had come for building new facilities and relocating from one side of the city where space had become crowded to the site anticipated years before.

During the process of construction, preparation, and location there were challenges of various dimensions. There were delays and unexpected requirements and a host of other experiences  in which many of us allowed ourselves to become somewhat frustrated. We became impatient and wanted so much to move forward to our new location.

A wise deacon council exercised their responsibilities quite well. One of our deacons expressed the sentients of men ordained to serve: "Be patient. When we are there [in the new buildings] we will be so joyous the frustrated feelings of the current times will hardly be remembered."

The words of the song many of us remember singing so often through the years entitled *When We All Get to Heaven* should encourage us all as we patiently work and walk and wait for our coming joys of Heaven.

*Just one glimpse of Him in glory*

*Will the toils of life repay. [Refrain]*


*4. Onward to the prize before us!*

*Soon His beauty we'll behold;*

*Soon the pearly gates will open—*

*We shall tread the streets of gold. [Refrain]*


*— Eliza E. Hewitt*

# 10. Destined for Deeper Relationships

# 11. Managing the Misconceptions and Clarifying Expectations

**Main idea: Since we study Heaven so little, misconceptions abound. However, Heaven will be the most fulfilling experience— and it won't end. In fact, it will continue getting better and better the longer it lasts.**

*To be in resurrected bodies on a resurrected earth in resurrected friendships, enjoying a resurrected culture with the resurrected Jesus— now that will be the ultimate party! Everybody will be who God made them to be— and none of us will suffer or die again.*

*As a Christian, the day I die will be the best day I've ever lived. But it won't be the best day I ever will live.  Resurrection day will be far better. And  the first day on the New Earth— that will be one big step for mankind, one giant leap for God's glory.*

*— Randy Alcorn[63]*

[63] *Heaven*, page 458

# A. Three misconceptions about Heaven

**There are some strange ideas that must be surfaced and dispelled about Heaven**. It is actually ironic that the most wonderful, most exciting, most fulfilling place ever conceived would have such strange ideas circulated about it.

Here are three.

1. **Misconception #1 = God is a cosmic killjoy.**

   The Creator of Heaven and Earth is eternally good, exciting, innovative, beautiful, fascinating, participative, enjoyable, and refreshing. We could exhaust our dictionaries in all languages and still would have been unable to begin a worthy description of the infinite, self-existent, immutable, immense, eternal God.

   If a person simply looks at the magnitude and the mystery of the universe objectively, he or she must conclude that this God who loves the world He created from nothing is remarkable beyond all description. For such a person to be boring or a destroyer of joy is unimaginable.

2. **Misconception #2 = Heaven will be monotonous, routine, and boring.**

   Sometimes people complain that they are bored. In response to such a remark, others have retorted that "only boring people get bored."

   In the world in which we currently live there are far too many options for us to be bored.

   But wait…

Heaven is going to be infinitely more remarkable than this old earth. Yet there is also another perspective articulated by G.K. Chesterton indicating that even monotony doesn't have to be boring.

> *A child kicks his legs rhythmically through excess, not absence, of life. Because children have abounding vitality, because they are in spirit fierce and free, therefore they want things repeated and unchanged.*
>
> *They always say, "Do it again"; and the grown up person does it again until he is nearly dead. For grown-up people are not strong enough to exult in monotony.*
>
> *But perhaps God is strong enough to exult in monotony.*
>
> *It is possible that God says every morning, "Do it again" to the sun; and every evening, "Do it again" to the moon…*
>
> *It may be that he has the eternal appetite of infancy; for we have sinned and grown old, and our Father is younger than we.*[64]

The happenings and activities of Heaven will not be boring or monotonous.

We will be renewed and say, "Thank you, Father, for the new joys every day" and from time to time "Do it again, Father."

And, I think He will.

3. **Misconception #3 = Heaven will be one long church service.**

While worship will be the central activity in a God-centered New Heaven and New Earth, it will not be *the only* activity.

We will completely realize that worship that touches all of life happens in other places than simply in the gatherings specifically focused on singing.

---

[64] Quoted by Robert Jeffress in *A Place Called Heaven*, page 101

Such worship helps us to see that God can and will be glorified in regular and routine service as well as what we call a worship service.

In other words, our definition of worship is far too narrow.

1 Corinthians 10:31—

*So whether you eat or drink or **whatever you do**, do it all for the glory of God.*

Colossians 3:23-24—

*Whatever you do, **work at it with all your heart,** as working for the Lord, not for human masters, since you know that you will receive an inheritance from the Lord as a reward. **It is the Lord Christ you are serving.***

The specific worship services in which we will be involved will be the most exhilarating we have ever experienced. Revelation 4, Revelation 5 , and Revelation 7 give us a marvelous foretaste. Reviewing Isaiah 6:1-4 is beneficial.

(We'll talk more about worship in the following lesson.)

MANAGING THE
MISCONCEPTIONS

1. **RESTRICTIVE**
   — WE WILL EXPERIENCE ULTIMATE FREEDOM

2. **ROUTINE & BORING**
   — WE WILL CONTINUE LEARNING AND GROWING

3. **ONE LONG CHURCH SERVICE**
   — OUR DEFINITION OF WORSHIP IS TOO NARROW

# B. If not that, then what...?

If Heaven won't be "all of that," then what will it be?

What will life be like?

Paul Enns offers twelve beneficial observations.[65]

1.  **Joy and Happiness await in Heaven.**

    Happiness on the present Earth seems to come and go and is attached often to certain life experiences. We get a raise, or a special recognition, or score a game-winning home run, or win a trip to a desired place, and we feel momentarily "happy."

    At best, those events or occasions are limited in duration.

    The New Heaven and New Earth will involve us in constant, unending joy and happiness that is literally permanent and unending.

    Isaiah 51:11—

    *Those the Lord has rescued will return.*

    *They will enter Zion with singing;* ***everlasting joy will crown their heads.***

    *Gladness and joy will overtake them, and* ***sorrow and sighing will flee away.***

    Isaiah 52:9-10—

    ***Burst into songs of joy together,*** *you ruins of Jerusalem, for the Lord has comforted his people, he has redeemed Jerusalem.*

---

[65] See *Heaven Revealed*, page 121 and following.

> *The Lord will lay bare his holy arm in the sight of all the nations, and all the ends of the earth will see the salvation of our God.*

God actually created man and woman for joy and happiness. In all the many activities in which we become involved in Heaven our lives will be characteristically joyful.

The context of the New Heaven and New Earth indicates how infinitely joyful we will be.

Isaiah 65:17-25—

> *See, I will create new heavens and a new earth.*
>
> *The former things will not be remembered, nor will they come to mind.*
>
> *But be glad and rejoice forever in what I will create, for **I will create Jerusalem to be a delight and its people a joy.***
>
> *I will rejoice over Jerusalem and take delight in my people; the sound of weeping and of crying will be heard in it no more.*
>
> *Never again will there be in it an infant who lives but a few days, or an old man who does not live out his years; the one who dies at a hundred will be thought a mere child; the one who fails to reach a hundred will be considered accursed.*
>
> *They will build houses and dwell in them; they will plant vineyards and eat their fruit.*
>
> *No longer will they build houses and others live in them, or plant and others eat.*
>
> *For as the days of a tree, so will be the days of my people; my chosen ones will long enjoy the work of their hands.*

*They will not labor in vain, nor will they bear children doomed to misfortune; for they will be a people blessed by the Lord, they and their descendants with them.*

*Before they call I will answer; while they are still speaking I will hear.*

*The wolf and the lamb will feed together, and the lion will eat straw like the ox, and dust will be the serpent's food.*

*They will neither harm nor destroy on all my holy mountain…*

The presence of the Lord Himself will be the central focus of our joy and gladness.

Zechariah 2:10-13—

**"Shout and be glad, Daughter Zion. For I am coming,** *and I will live among you," declares the Lord. "Many nations will be joined with the Lord in that day and will become my people. I will live among you and you will know that the Lord Almighty has sent me to you. The Lord will inherit Judah as his portion in the holy land and will again choose Jerusalem. Be still before the Lord, all mankind, because he has roused himself from his holy dwelling."*

The Triune God is by far and away (into infinity) the most fascinating person(s) in the universe. Learning about and relating to Him without hindrance or barrier will indeed bring unspeakable joy, happiness, and fulfillment throughout the ages to come.

## 2. Restored health awaits us, as well.

Fanny Crosby's story shows us an example of what awaits for us in Heaven.[66]

---

[66] Randy Alcorn, *Heaven,* page 439.

She was only six weeks old when a man who *claimed to be* a physician placed a hot poultice on her eyes. The effort to treat an eye infection with such limited medical knowledge resulted in almost-immediate blindness for the child.

She never regained her eyesight, yet became a prolific hymn writer and memorizer of Scripture.

Beginning in 1864 Fanny began to compose hymns. She ultimately wrote between 5,500 and 9,000 hymns. (To preserve her modesty she assumed as many as 200 other names to attach to her authorship.)

A time-honored statement attributed to Fanny— who lived to age 95 — goes something like this:

> If I had a choice, I would still choose to remain blind, because when I get to Heaven, the first face that shall ever gladden my sight will be that of my Savior.

Notice what the Bible says about blindness— and all other health concerns.

Isaiah 35:5-6—

> Then will the eyes of the blind be opened and the ears of the deaf unstopped. Then will the lame leap like a deer, and the mute tongue shout for joy. Water will gush forth in the wilderness and streams in the desert.

Here's another way to think about our health in Heaven…

The "nos" of what will be in Heaven are good indicators for us that can be turned into positives of our understanding of how glorious Heaven will be.

- No death

- No suffering

- No funeral homes

- No abortion clinics

- No psychiatric wards

- No rape

- No drug rehabilitation centers

- No worry

- No depression

- No mourning

- No pain

- No arthritis

- No handicaps

- No cancer

- No drunkenness

- No accidents

- No mental illness

- No hungry people unsatisfied

- No weeping

- No illness

- No _____ [fill in the blank]

We could go on and on…

Our senses will be perfect and, who knows, our Father God may endow us with additional sense capacities by which we can perceive our environment.

KNOWING WHAT'S CERTAINLY

# NOT THERE

PROVIDES CLARITY AS TO WHAT

# IS THERE

Our health will not deteriorate and we probably will never reach a peak of our healthy abilities.

Isaiah 29:18–

> In that day the deaf will hear the words of the scroll, and **out of gloom and darkness** the eyes of the blind will see.

Isaiah 32:3-4–

> Then the eyes of those who see will no longer be closed, and the ears of those who hear will listen. **The fearful heart will know and understand**, and the stammering tongue will be fluent and clear.

Again, knowing what certainly is *not there* provides clarity as to what is there — which leads us to our next observation.

3. **Prosperity and security are available to everyone in Heaven.**

The peaceful contentment of the days to come is typified by the declaration of the Lord Almighty in Zechariah 3:10, "In that day each of you will invite your neighbor to sit under your vine and fig tree."

Peace and blessing will be the benefits bestowed without measure from our Creator, Redeemer, and Sustainer.

There have been only a limited number of days on the fallen Earth, where we now reside, to be in a place where there is unending prosperity, peace, and the absence of conflict and war.  This will be a new experience for us in the New Heaven and the New Earth.

The fact that all war and conflict will have ended and will never come again will be a joyful experience, yet probably one which may take some time of realization to fully enjoy to the extent that God intends.

The words of David Jeremiah which became a title of one of his many books expresses the feeling of many of us: *I Never Thought I'd See the Day.*[67]

In the book he expresses his sincere concern about the decline of  our culture with insightful clarity.

The title of the book can be *reversed and rewritten* when we experience Heaven. *Every Day is a Victory* when you spend it in the presence of the Lord.

### 4.  Peace and safety will be unfailing.

Not only will wars and conflicts among men be absent, there will also be peace between mankind and animals. God gave man dominion over all animals and placed the fear of man in animals.

Genesis 9:2—

> *The fear and dread of you will fall on all the beasts of the earth, and on all the birds in the sky, on every creature that moves along the ground, and on all the fish in the sea; they are given into your hands.*

---

[67] Jeremiah, *I Never Thought I'd See the Day.*

Hosea 2:18—

*In that day I will make a covenant for them with the beasts of the field, the birds in the sky and the creatures that move along the ground.*

*Bow and sword and battle I will abolish from the land, so that **all may lie down in safety.***

In Isaiah 65, we read the reference about God creating the New heaven and the New Earth.

Isaiah 65:17,25—

*See, I will create new heavens and a new earth. The former things will not be remembered, nor will they come to mind…*

***The wolf and the lamb will feed together, and the lion will eat straw like the ox, and dust will be the serpent's food.***

***They will neither harm nor destroy on all my holy mountain…***

The conditions of Paradise in the Garden of Eden which were lost to mankind will be restored as a Paradise regained.

In every area of life, we can agree with what Paul Enns wrote—

*What Adam lost, Christ will regain.*[68]

## 5. We will not feel sad, cry, mourn, or face death.

God has graciously promised that there will be a glorious future day when we will be free from the pain of loss which is still part of our lives here on old Earth. In the New Heaven and the New Earth things change.

---

[68] Enns, *Heaven Revealed*, page 129

Revelation 21:4—

> *He will wipe away every tear from their eyes; and there will no longer be any death;* **there will no longer be any mourning, or crying, or pain;** *the first things have passed away.*

The accomplishment of our Lord Jesus with His death and Resurrection resulted in the defeat of mankind's greatest enemy, death.

Isaiah's prophecy will be fulfilled.

Isaiah 25:8—

> *He will swallow up death forever. The Sovereign Lord will* **wipe away the tears from all faces; He will remove His people's disgrace from all the earth.** *The Lord has spoken.*

A day of eternal joy, peace, and tranquility also indicated by Jesus in the Sermon on the Mount in Matthew 5:4 will be realized.

Matthew 5:4—

> *Blessed are those who mourn, for* **they will be comforted***.*

## 6. We will recognize and relate to each other.

Jesus promised His disciples He would see them— and know them— in the future.

Matthew 26:29—

> *"I tell you, I will not drink from this fruit of the vine from now on until that day when I drink it new with you in my Father's Kingdom."*

Paul Enns indicates that because Jesus spoke of "I" and "you" that He implied there would be continuity in both Himself and the disciples. They would recognize-- and know— each other. He would recognize them and they would recognize Him.[69]

We will be identified by our individual personalities and appearances. John 3:16 promises that we receive eternal life as individual believers. We are and will be the "whosoevers" that are recognizable by those who know us and those whom we know.[70]

Randy Alcorn clarifies the identity and recognition concern.[71]

> What makes you "you"?

> It's not only your body but also your memory, personality traits, gifts, passions, preferences, and interests.

> In the final resurrection I believe all these facets will be restored and amplified, untarnished by sin and the curse.

## 7. Our resurrected bodies will be locked into an appropriate age.

Before the Fall of man into sin and all the results that were set into action, we can safely assume that Adam and Eve were "perfect." They were young, sinless, and without flaw.

That would mean that they were breathtakingly beautiful. It was with the Fall that the deterioration of the human body began.

When we receive our resurrection bodies we will have that which God desired for us from prior to the beginning in Genesis.

Saint Augustine, a historical theologian, said the following about our bodies:

---

[69] Enns, *Heaven Revealed*, page 131

[70] Review lesson 10 for more about relationships.

[71] Randy Alcorn, *Heaven*, page 282

*… [our bodies] shall be of that size which it had either attained or should have attained in the flower of its youth, and shall enjoy the beauty that arises from preserving symmetry and proportion in all its members.*[72]

Hank Hanegraaff, a modern Bible scholar, says—

*Our DNA is programmed in such a way, at a particular point, we reach optimal development from a functional perspective. For the most part, it appears that we reach this age somewhere in our twenties and thirties…*

*If the blueprints for our glorified bodies are in the DNA, then it would stand to reason that our bodies will be resurrected at the optimal stage of development determined by our DNA.*[73]

8. **Our perception of family members will be uniquely appropriate.**

If all persons in the New Heaven are uniquely at a peak age of development in terms of physical abilities, what happens in regard to our family relationships?

What about those who were our fathers and mothers, grandfathers and grandmothers, and even further back in our respective family trees?

What about our children and their children and the children of their children?

How will we relate to them?

The principle of continuity expressed so definitively by Randy Alcorn indicates that we will pick up where we left off on the present Earth and find even deeper and fuller ways to relate in Heaven. We will not cease being who we are and become other persons.

---

[72] See The City of God, 22:19,2, quoted by Paul Enns.

[73] Hank Hanegraaff, *Resurrection*, pages.134-135, referenced by Paul Enns.

That same reality extends to the familial and friendship relationships which we treasured so highly while on the present Earth.[74]

What about marriage in Heaven?

Jesus clearly stated in response to questions being asked of Him by the Sadducees, "At the resurrection people will neither marry nor be given in marriage; they will be like the angels in heaven" (Matthew 22:30).

(We addressed this in lesson 10.)

Actually, there will be one absolutely unique and different marriage in Heaven between Christ and His Bride, the Church.

Paul presents the concept and connection of human marriage and the higher and greater reality it illuminates.

> Ephesians 5:32-33—

> *This is a profound mystery—but **I am talking about Christ and the church.***

> *However, each one of you also must love his wife as he loves himself, and the wife must respect her husband.*

The reality of married couples who have close intimacy physically and emotionally will deepen those exciting bonds. Even though the institution of human marriage will end because the purpose for it will have been fulfilled, continuity of friendship will be a reality that we can enjoy throughout eternity.

Married couples who have become best friends will certainly not reject their friends in Heaven.

What about the sexual relationship of married couples?

---

[74] See his book *Heaven*, particularly chapter 35, pages 349-358.

Randy Alcorn expresses this well-studied idea well.[75]

> *… since there is a different sort of continuity between earthly marriage and the marriage of Christ to his church, there may also be some way in which the intimacy and pleasure we now know as sex will also be fulfilled in some higher form.*
>
> *I don't know what that would be, but I do know that sex was designed by God, and I don't expect him to discard it without replacing it with something better.*

9. **We will work… and it will be fulfilling.**

The two primary responsibilities of Man in the Garden of Eden were worship and work.

Genesis 2:15—

> *The Lord God took the man and put him in the Garden of Eden **to work it and take care of it.***

Our Beloved Creator is also a worker. He worked in the perfect world that He created, and He continues to work in the world after sin has entered and caused the fall of that creation.

John 5:17—

> *In his defense Jesus said to them, **"My Father is always at his work to this very day, and I too am working.**"*

It is obvious that work is not a "curse" from God as a result of sin.

The problem that work has become for us came as a result of the penalty enacted on all of Creation, the Fall of Earth, as well as man.

---

[75] Alcorn, *Heaven*, page 352

# WORK ISN'T A RESULT OF THE FALL- TOIL IS

Genesis 3:17—

> *To Adam he said, "Because you listened to your wife and ate fruit from the tree about which I commanded you, 'You must not eat from it,' cursed is the ground because of you; through painful toil you will eat food from it all the days of your life…"*

When the New Heaven and the New Earth is created for us and our abode throughout eternity, the curse on the ground and the difficulty of work because of that curse will be removed. Work will again become the joyful, fulfilling, purposeful activity that God intended for it to be.

Some Scripture reading can help us understand the value and importance of work.

2 Corinthians 9:8—

> *And God is able to bless you abundantly, so that in all things at all times, having all that you need, **you will abound in every good work.***

Colossians 3:23–

*Whatever you do, **work at it with all your heart, as working for the Lord**, not for human masters…*

Colossians 4:17—

*Tell Archippus: "See to it that you **complete the ministry you have received in the Lord**."*

2 Timothy 2:21—

*Those who cleanse themselves from the latter will be instruments for special purposes, made holy, useful to the Master and **prepared to do any good work**.*

Titus 1:7—

*Since an overseer **manages God's household**, he must be blameless—not overbearing, not quick-tempered, not given to drunkenness, not violent, not pursuing dishonest gain.*

Hebrews 13:17—

*Have confidence in your leaders and submit to their authority, because they keep watch over you as those who must give an account. Do this so that **their work will be a joy, not a burden**, for that would be of no benefit to you.*

1 Peter 1:17—

*Since you call on a Father **who judges each person's work impartially**, live out your time as foreigners here in reverent fear.*

Revelation 2:2—

***I know your deeds, your hard work and your perseverance.** I know that you cannot tolerate wicked people, that you have tested those who claim to be apostles but are not, and have found them false.*

This will not be diminished in Heaven, but redeemed and enhanced.

## 10. We will be playful and active.

The affection that Jesus our Lord (who is the God/Man) expressed is obvious when you read through the New Testament.

Mark 10:13-15—

> People were bringing little children to Jesus for Him to place His hands on them, but the disciples rebuked them. When Jesus saw this, He was indignant.
>
> He said to them, "Let the little children come to Me, and do not hinder them, for the Kingdom of God belongs to such as these. Truly I tell you, **anyone who will not receive the Kingdom of God like a little child will never enter it.**"

Jesus knew that children need to be given freedom to be children. We are called the children of God. So, I believe that there will be time for playing in Heaven.

I am personally thrilled that the likelihood of play will be available in Heaven. I like to play and always have liked to play. I believe I will still be able to have times of play in Heaven.

I also believe that we will probably exercise in continuity of the joy and release that many of us experience now when we exercise. The idea of sitting around and doing nothing all the time can become very boring and Heaven will not be boring. We are created to be active and in our resurrection bodies It seems quite logical that we will be active in ways that are appropriate.

Another related aspect of these involvements is that we will laugh.

Luke 6:21,23—

> *Blessed are you when you hunger now, for you will be satisfied. Blessed are you who weep now, **for you will laugh...***
>
> ***Rejoice in that day and leap for joy, because great is your reward in heaven.***

Leaping for joy seems to indicate laughing. Sam Storms envisions it like this:

> *The happiness of Heaven is not like the steady, placid state of a mountain lake where barely a ripple disturbs the tranquility of its water. Heaven is more akin to the surging, swelling waves of the Mississippi at flood stage.*[76]

Do you enjoy laughing?

Do you participate in smiling?

Even though I think some people may draw a line at "leaping for joy," perhaps we will all have the energy and enthusiasm to do so in Heaven. We are going to experience glorious moments of release and happiness in our future.

## 11. We will have individual dwellings (homes).

Many of us are familiar with the promises Jesus makes in John 14:1-3.

John 14:1-3—

> *Do not let your hearts be troubled. You believe in God; believe also in me. My Father's house has many rooms; if that were not so, would I have told you that I am going there to prepare a place for you?*

---

[76] Sam Storms, quoted by Randy Alcorn, in *Heaven*, page 425

*And if I go and prepare a place for you, I will come back and take you to be with me that you also may be where I am.*

The passage reveals the importance of several terms—

- Father's house

- Many rooms

- A place for you

- Where I am

The indication of these terms suggests that Heaven is a place that will be both spacious and intimate, cozy but wide and open.

New Testament Scholar D.A. Carson suggests—

*Since heaven is here pictured as the Father's house, it is more natural to think of "dwelling- places" within a house as rooms or suites…*

*The simplest explanation is best: my Father's house refers to Heaven, and in Heaven are many rooms, many dwelling-places. The point is not the lavishness of each apartment, but the fact that such ample provision has been made that there is more than enough space for every one of Jesus' disciples to join him in his Father's home.[77]*

"Home" is a special place with various shades of meaning that all refer at various times to the place(s) we call "Home."

- We sometimes refer to our country, our state, our area, our city, our neighborhood, our street, our place, or our room(s).

- Family, friends, neighbors, church, and community all are part of "Home" and the experience of "Home."

---

[77] Quoted in Alcorn's book *Heaven*, page 333

- Our ultimate Home will be the place our Lord has prepared for us on the New Heaven and the New Earth.

## 12. We will enjoy fellowship meals, banquets, significant feasts, and special suppers.

While the celebration is inaugurated with the beginning of the Millennial Kingdom, it will continue into the eternal state of the New Heavens and New Earth. The words of Revelation 19:9 should resonate with all of us.

Revelation 19:9—

> Then the Angel said to me, "Write this: **Blessed are those who are invited to the wedding supper** of the Lamb!"
>
> And he added, "These are the true words of God."

The Scriptures seem to be replete with expressions and events that include eating and fellowship around tables. **The words for *eating*, *meals*, and *food* appear more than one thousand times in Scripture with the word for *feast* adding another 187 times.**

JESUS SPENT
MORE TIME
AROUND A TABLE
THAN HE DID AT
THE TEMPLE.

The picture we see in God's account of His self-revelation is that He endorses the joyful merriment and, on the other hand, the spiritual focus that comes to pass in appropriate gatherings where food is enjoyed.

The Jewish Feasts, the Passover, the Lord's Supper, the Marriage Supper of the Lamb, and the parables of our Lord Jesus are only a few illustrations of the important experiences enjoyed and lessons learned at special meals.

An informed case can be certainly made that with the expectation of the principle of continuity in the New Heaven and the New Earth, there will numerous opportunities for us to enjoy and to be informed by the meals we will be having in Heaven.

Jesus made a point of eating and drinking with His disciples after His resurrection. This was one of the first things He did!

Luke 24:40-43—

*When he had said this, he showed them his hands and feet.*

*And while they still did not believe it because of joy and amazement, he asked them, "Do you have anything here to eat?"*

*They gave him a piece of broiled fish, and he took it and ate it in their presence.*

John 21:10-15—

*Jesus said to them, "Bring some of the fish you have just caught."*

*So Simon Peter climbed back into the boat and dragged the net ashore. It was full of large fish, 153, but even with so many the net was not torn.*

*Jesus said to them, "Come and have breakfast."*

*None of the disciples dared ask him, "Who are you?" They knew it was the Lord.*

> *Jesus came, **took the bread and gave it to them, and did the same with the fish. This was now the third time Jesus appeared to his disciples after he was raised from the dead.***
>
> *When they had finished eating, Jesus said to Simon Peter, "Simon son of John, do you love me more than these?"*
>
> *"Yes, Lord," he said, "you know that I love you."*
>
> *Jesus said, **"Feed my lambs."***

Acts 10:39-41—

> *We are witnesses of everything he did in the country of the Jews and in Jerusalem. They killed him by hanging him on a cross, but God raised him from the dead on the third day and caused him to be seen.*
>
> *He was not seen by all the people, but by witnesses whom God had already chosen—by us **who ate and drank with him after he rose from the dead.***

Paul indicated by inspired instruction—

1 Corinthians 10:31—

> **So whether you eat or drink or whatever you do, do it all for the glory of God.**

Glorifying God will be our primary joy in Heaven and that certainly will include in the way we participate in feasts, fellowships, and special suppers.

We should not omit repeating the prophecy of Isaiah regarding a time to come in the Kingdom of God. **The abundant banquet pictured in Isaiah helps us to realize more fully what God has in store for those who love Him.**

Isaiah 25:6-8—

*On this mountain **the Lord Almighty will prepare a feast of rich food for all peoples, a banquet** of aged wine— the best of meats and the finest of wines.*

*On this mountain He will destroy the shroud that enfolds all peoples, the sheet that covers all nations; He will swallow up death forever.*

*The Sovereign Lord will wipe away the tears from all faces; He will remove His people's disgrace from all the earth.*

*The Lord has spoken.*

# C. Always growing and learning and experiencing more

Some of the best news is that we "never arrive" in the Kingdom. Or, to say it a better way— **we've simultaneously arrived and we're always seeing more unfolding revelation.**

You may have heard someone say, "We may not understand now, but in Heaven we will understand and know everything."

That is not actually a true statement. God, Himself, is the only One knows everything.

We will know more than we do now, we will know more clearly, but we'll never know everything. Paul stated that as a man he knew in part, yet his statement "then I shall know fully, even as I am known" (1 Corinthians 13:12) bears clarification.

To "know fully" did not mean that he and we would become omniscient. His statement meant that we would know without error and misconception.

Because we will see God's face, we will know Him much more deeply and truly. Yet, God will still be infinite, and we will still be finite. While we will be flawless in Heaven, we must understand that not knowing everything does not mean we are flawed. We will actually spend eternity learning and coming to know more about God and the beautiful New Heaven and New Earth He has given for us to enjoy and experience.

Paul clarifies even more.

> Ephesians 2:6-7—
>
> > *And God raised us up with Christ and seated us with Him in the Heavenly realms in Christ Jesus, in order **that in the coming ages He might show the incomparable riches of His grace**, expressed in His kindness to us in Christ Jesus.*

Jonathan Edwards, the theologian-preacher, said **there will never be a time when there is no more glory of the glory of God for the redeemed to discover and enjoy.**

The infinite God is truly infinite.

We will be blessed throughout eternity learning more about Him and about the truths of His creation.

# D. Rest, refreshment, rejuvenation...

We realize that gliding around and floating on clouds while playing harps are not what we now expect as our primary Heaven activities. God has plans for us that are meaningful and fulfilling.

I am confident that we will rest *not* because of some of the difficulties and frailties of our old earth bodies. That does not mean that we will not rest.

After God finished creating the world, He, Himself, rested on the seventh day. He was not exhausted but paused to reflect on the accomplishments of the first six days and to establish a pattern for mankind then and in our current time as well.

Eden provides a vivid picture of rest. Eden was perfect yet a time was set aside for rest even there. In His Creation, God built into life the need to pause and to trust and to reflect and to believe.

One of the greatest problems we face at the time in which we live is the tyranny of the urgent.

The push and shove of daily life seems to be relentless. We have a deep need to be still and know that God is God.

The importance of the Biblical Sabbath can hardly be overstated.

Exodus 20:9-11—

*Six days you shall labor and do all your work, but the seventh day is a sabbath to the Lord your God. On it you shall not do any work, neither you, nor your son or daughter, nor your male or female servant, nor your animals, nor any foreigner residing in your towns. For in six days the Lord made the heavens and the earth, the sea, and all that is in them, but he rested on the seventh day. Therefore the Lord blessed the Sabbath day and made it holy.*

Leviticus 25:4-5—

*But in the seventh year the land is to have a year of sabbath rest, a sabbath to the Lord. Do not sow your fields or prune your vineyards. Do not reap what grows of itself or harvest the grapes of your untended vines. The land is to have a year of rest.*

Revelation 14:13—

*Then I heard a voice from heaven say, "Write this: Blessed are the dead who die in the Lord from now on."*

Hebrews 4:9-11—

***There remains, then, a Sabbath-rest for the people of God;** for anyone who enters God's rest also rests from their works, just as God did from his.*

*Let us, therefore, make every effort to enter that rest, so that no one will perish by following their example of disobedience.*

Jesus offered an invitation with a beautiful promise of rest attached.

Matthew 11:28-30—

*Come to me, all you who are weary and burdened, and I will give you rest. Take my yoke upon you and learn from me, for am gentle and humble in heart, and you will find rest for your souls. For my yoke is easy and my burden light.*

The rest Jesus promised far supersedes the relaxation needed by tired bodies. His rest involves us body, mind, soul, and spirit. The rest that awaits us in Heaven can be experienced even now by faith. And, that is indeed a foretaste of that perfect rest.

## 11. Managing the Misconceptions and Clarifying Expectations

# 12. Worship as a Way of Life— Then and Now

Main idea: Worship will be our way of life in Heaven (our definition of *worship* is far too narrow).  We began our study learning about how to plan for our ultimate destination. One of the best ways to prepare is to live now in the same way we'll live then— with worship as our way of life, living the prayer "on earth as it is in Heaven."

*Once we see God as He really is, no one will need to beg, threaten, or shame us into praising Him. We will overflow in gratitude and praise. We are created to worship God. There's no higher pleasure. At times we'll lose ourselves in praise, doing nothing but worshipping him. At other times we'll worship Him when we build a cabinet, paint a picture, cook a meal, talk with an old friend, take a walk, or throw a ball.*

*— Randy Alcorn*[78]

---

[78] *Heaven*, page 197

# A. A glimpse into the future

In Heaven we will have the remarkable privilege of participating in the infinite delight of the eternal relationship of the Triune Godhead. The wonder we observe being experienced in Revelation 4-5 among Heaven's inhabitants indicates an ever-growing and deepening appreciation of the greatness of God.

While most of God's people realize we will worship God in Heaven, we do not completely comprehend how thrilling that worship is going to be. The worship in Heaven will be all-encompassing. Helpful words of instruction are recorded throughout the final book of the Bible.

Revelation 5:13-14–

*Then **I heard every creature in heaven and on earth and under the earth and on the sea, and all that is in them**, saying: "To him who sits on the throne and to the Lamb be praise and honor and glory and power, for ever and ever!"*

*The four living creatures said, "Amen," and the elders fell down and worshiped.*

Revelation 7:9-12—

*After this I looked, and there before me was **a great multitude that no one could count, from every nation, tribe, people and language, standing before the throne and before the Lamb**. They were wearing white robes and were holding palm branches in their hands.*

*And they cried out in a loud voice: "Salvation belongs to our God, who sits on the throne, and to the Lamb."*

*All the angels were standing around the throne and around the elders and the four living creatures.*

*They fell down on their faces before the throne and worshiped God, saying: "Amen! Praise and glory and wisdom and thanks and honor and power and strength be to our God for ever and ever. Amen!"*

Revelation 21:3,22—

*And I heard a loud voice from the throne saying, "Look! God's dwelling place is now among the people, and he will dwell with them. They will be his people, and God himself will be with them and be their God…"*

*I did not see a temple in the city, because the Lord God Almighty and the Lamb are its temple.*

# B. Will we be involved in one long worship event?

Many of us learned— somewhere— that Heaven will be "one long church service." Hopefully, you've seen something broader over the course of our time together.[79]

But, while we're discussing the topic of worship, let's ask the question: Will Heaven be one long worship event?

The answer: "Yes and no."

We will not be forever and always simply bowing and stretched upon our faces worshipping God. The Scripture tells us that we will be doing other things such as living in dwellings, eating, drinking, reigning with Christ, gathering at feasts, standing, walking, and working for God.

**The Biblical perspective is that everything we do is a life of worship.** So, all of these things can— and will— be done in honor and gratitude to our Creator.

---

[79] We commented on this in misconception #3 in the previous chapter.

**That is, all that we do will ultimately be an act of worship.** We will live in unbroken relationship with Christ to the point that we will, at times, assemble with multitudes who are also worshipping Him.

Cornelius Venema said—

> *No legitimate activity of life— whether in marriage, family, business, play, friendship, education, politics, etc.,— escapes the claims of the Christ's kingship...*

> *Certainly those who live and reign with Christ forever will find the diversity and complexity of their worship of God not less but richer in the life to come.*

> *Every legitimate activity of new creaturely life will be included within the life of worship of God's people.*[80]

Because many of us are coming to realize that the most important activity in which we are involved on the present Earth is the worship of the one and only living God, we are not surprised that when we look forward, we are thrilled to know that worship of the living God in His fullness will be our most important activity on the New Heaven and New Earth as well. We are getting ready now as we look ahead to the purity of the worship in life and practice which will be ours then.

**We will learn more and more about God and we will be continually more and more fascinated by what we learn.** We are created to worship and we are restless unless we focus our attention in worship upon the only One who can truly satisfy our hearts, minds, and souls.

In Heaven we will not be distracted as we often are on earth during worship. The thrill of knowing God, better and better, more and more, throughout eternity is the delight we will have forever and ever.

## Theologian J.I. Packer expressed it well.[81]

---

[80] Quoted by Randy Alcorn, *Heaven*, page 196.

[81] Quoted by Randy Alcorn, *Heaven*, page 198.

*Hearts on earth may say in the course of a joyful experience, "I don't want this to ever end."*

*But invariably it does.*

*The heart of those in Heaven say, "I want this to go on forever."*

*And it will.*

*There is no better news than this.*

# C. The throne remains the center.

### What is the place of worship revealed in Heaven to John?

Revelation 4:1 tells us that the Apostle John was allowed to look through an open door into Heaven and to behold a remarkable sight. In these extraordinary moments John was permitted to view worship occurring in Heaven.

The Angelic hosts were getting ready for the final events leading up to our Lord Jesus Christ's return.

Revelation 4:1-3—

*After this I looked, and there before me was a door standing open in heaven.*

*And the voice I had first heard speaking to me like a trumpet said, "Come up here, and I will show you what must take place after this."*

*At once I was in the Spirit, and there before me was a throne in heaven with someone sitting on it.*

*And the one who sat there had the appearance of jasper and ruby. A rainbow that shone like an emerald encircled the throne…*

That said, the throne remains the center of worship.

Or, to say it another way, a life of worship flows from what happens when we're at the throne.

We get a very special look into heaven that will occur around the throne of God at a great worship service.

1.  **Many scholars regard Revelation 4 and Revelation 5 as the greatest exposition on the subject of worship found in the Bible.**

    Vernon M. Whatley observes—

    > *Notice that no one in these passages seems to be under compulsion to worship God. No one is standing there, cracking the whip and demanding veneration. The whole of heaven is rejoicing voluntarily and from the heart.*
    >
    > *Why?*
    >
    > *Because they know that Jesus Christ is no longer that baby in a manger, represented by so many cracked and peeling images in Nativity sets the world over.*
    >
    > *Neither is he the bleeding and broken "criminal," humbled and half-naked on a cross, the victim of those who thought they were bigger than Him.*
    >
    > *And He's not the cold and mangled corpse that once lay in a borrowed tomb either.*
    >
    > *Those whose praises fill the heavens know that Jesus Christ is exalted. He is all in all, and heaven's inhabitants never tire of worshipping him.*
    >
    > *Neither will we. You and I will never run out of things to thank him for, and praising him will never become boring.* [82]

---

[82] From Vernon M. Whatley's *Called to Worship,* quoted in David Jeremiah's *The Book of Signs*, pages 220-221.

2.  **Revelation 4:2-3 indicates the key word of these verses to be a word repeated 42 times in Revelation, *throne*. Everything flows from the throne.**

The word *throne* is emphasized in these two chapters.

Revelation 4:2—

> *At once I was in the Spirit, and there before me was a **throne** in heaven with someone sitting on it.*

Revelation 4:3—

> *And the one who sat there had the appearance of jasper and ruby. A rainbow that shone like an emerald encircled the **throne**.*

Revelation 4:5 (the word appears twice)—

> *From the **throne** came flashes of lightning, rumblings and peals of thunder. In front of the **throne**, seven lamps were blazing. These are the seven spirits of God.*

Revelation 4:6—

> *Also in front of the **throne** there was what looked like a sea of glass, clear as crystal.*

Revelation 4:10 (again, the word appears twice)—

> *… the twenty-four elders fall down before him who sits on the **throne** and worship him who lives for ever and ever. They lay their crowns before the **throne**…*

Revelation 5:11—

> *Then I looked and heard the voice of many angels, numbering thousands upon thousands, and ten thousand times ten thousand. They encircled the **throne** and the living creatures and the elders.*

Revelation 5:13—

> Then I heard every creature in heaven and on earth and under the
> earth and on the sea, and all that is in them, saying: "To him who sits
> on the **throne** and to the Lamb be praise and honor and glory and
> power, for ever and ever!"

3. **The heavenly throne of God testifies to His sovereignty,
   authority, reign, and His absolute power over all.**

   All that John could comprehend was the diamond-like brilliance, the
   gemstone-like beauty, and the stormy grandeur of the throne of God. God is
   seated there in unmatched brilliance, beauty, and power, yet in grace as well
   as glory.[83] God is to be now and always the focus of worthy worship.

4. **In Revelation 5 the scene expands to include not only God the
   Father but God the Son.**

   Around the throne were the 24 elders representative of the Church of the
   Living God. All the redeemed of all the ages will be there singing God's
   praises. Notice verses 8-10.

   Revelation 5:8-10—

   > And when he had taken it, the four living creatures and the twenty-
   > four elders fell down before the Lamb. Each one had a harp and they
   > were holding golden bowls full of incense, which are the prayers of
   > God's people.
   >
   > And they sang a new song, saying: "You are worthy to take the
   > scroll and to open its seals, because you were slain, and with your

---

[83] See David Jeremiah's *The Book of Signs*.

*blood you purchased for God persons from every tribe and language and people and nation."*

*"You have made them to be a kingdom and priests to serve our God, and they will reign on the earth."*

5.  **There seems to be a growing crescendo with a steady increase in volume and strength.**

Notice the rising number of doxologies (studies of praise to God).

- Revelation 1:6 = **two-fold doxology** = glory + power

- Revelation 4:11 = **three-fold doxology** = glory + power + honor

- Revelation 5:13 = **four-fold doxology** = glory + power + honor + praise

- Revelation 7:12 = **seven-fold doxology** = glory + power + honor + praise + wisdom + thanks + strength

Notice the text—

Revelation 1:6—

*… and has made us to be a kingdom and priests to serve his God and Father—to him be **glory and power** for ever and ever! Amen.*

Revelation 4:11—

*You are worthy, our Lord and God, to receive **glory and honor and power**, for you created all things, and by your will they were created and have their being.*

Revelation 5:13—

> *Then I heard every creature in heaven and on earth and under the earth and on the sea, and all that is in them, saying: "To him who sits on the throne and to the Lamb be **praise and honor and glory and power**, for ever and ever!"*

Revelation 7:11-12—

> *All the angels were standing around the throne and around the elders and the four living creatures.*
>
> *They fell down on their faces before the throne and worshiped God, saying: "Amen! **Praise and glory and wisdom and thanks and honor and power and strength** be to our God for ever and ever. Amen!"*

The solemn experience of seeking to remain personally controlled and without passion does not seem to be characteristic of what we see in these verses. What should this tell us about our personal engagement in expressing our heartfelt emotion in our praise of God— especially as we continue seeing more and more revelation of Who He is unfolding before us?

6. **What is revealed in John's experience regarding the contrast of present Earth and Heaven?**

John was living on the Isle of Patmos in exile. He was concerned about the persecution of the church enacted by the Roman Emperor, Domitian. God saw fit to open the door of Heaven so John could vividly see that there was something far better than any person could dream or imagine coming to those who are in Christ Jesus.

Worship made it possible for John to understand that even in the midst of discouragement and distress, God has made and is making a way to joy, confidence, and peace that surpasses understanding. God allowed John to see into the control room of the universe in order to see the future that God has planned for His people.

Worship takes us beyond the current reality to the promised and guaranteed reality that will transpire.

# D. Four worship principles revealed in God's Word

Here is our practical application as we close this lesson.

### 1. Worship is not about us; worship is about God.

We must be consistently focused not so much on the style of worship as our focus in worship.

Personal preferences are not as important as focus in the moments of private and corporate worship.

Our "whole self" must be in tune with God:

- Mind's attention

- Heart's affection

- Willful devotion

- Personal decision

The most well-known definition of *worship* outside the Word of God was penned by Archbishop William Temple.

*To worship is to quicken the conscience by the Holiness of God, to feed the mind with the Truth of God, to purge the imagination by the Beauty of God, to open the heart to the Love of God, to devote the will to the Purpose of God.*

2. **Worship is not so much about here as it is about there.**

We must adjust our thinking and affection on what is "there" because worship is the connection between us and God in the present time.

Colossians 3:1-4—

*Since, then, you have been raised with Christ, **set your hearts on things above**, where Christ is, seated at the right hand of God. **Set your minds on things above**, not on earthly things.*

*For you died, and your life is now hidden with Christ in God. When Christ, who is your life, appears, then you also will appear with him in glory.*

1 John 2:15-17—

***Do not love the world or anything in the world.** If anyone loves the world, love for the Father is not in them.*

*For everything in the world—the lust of the flesh, the lust of the eyes, and the pride of life—comes not from the Father but from the world.*

***The world and its desires pass away**, but whoever does the will of God lives forever.*

Even though worship is not so much about "here" as it is "there," we can affirm the following principle…

3. **Worship helps us to realize that our "now" is not as important as our "then."**

2 Corinthians 4:16-18—

*Therefore we do not lose heart. Though outwardly we are wasting away, yet inwardly we are being renewed day by day. For our light and momentary troubles are achieving for us an eternal glory that far outweighs them all.*

***So we fix our eyes not on what is seen, but what is unseen, since what is seen is temporary, but what is unseen is eternal.***

## THE FIRST THREE PRINCIPLES OF WORSHIP

 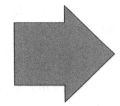 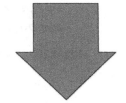

| 1. Look up— it's for God, not us | 2. Look ahead— it's about the future | 3. Live present— it also affects us now |

| Now | Then |
| --- | --- |
| Outward man wasting away | Inward man renewed day by day |
| Light affliction = today's troubles | Eternal glory = tomorrow's promise |
| Things seen = temporary | Things unseen = eternal |

4.  **Worship should be both private and public.**

John viewed worship in Heaven that involved many worshippers around the throne of God.

> Revelation 5:11-12—
>
> *Then I looked and heard the voice of many angels, **numbering thousands upon thousands, and 10,000 times 10,000.***
>
> *They encircled the throne and the living creatures and the elders. In a loud voice they were saying: **"Worthy is the Lamb, who was slain, to receive power and wealth and wisdom and strength and honor and glory and praise!"***
>
> Revelation 19:6-7—
>
> *Then I heard **what sounded like a great multitude**, like the roar of rushing waters and like loud peals of thunder, shouting: **"Hallelujah! For our Lord God Almighty reigns**. Let us rejoice and be glad and give him glory! For the wedding of the lamb has come, and his bride has made herself ready.*

This time is coming.

The big question is whether or not we are ready.

It is time now to prepare and to say with all:

# Amen.
# Come Lord Jesus!

# Resources

# Plus Ultra

We have considered a large number of issues regarding Heaven. If we go back over what we have considered in summary, we will probably have a large number of questions and needs for clarification.

There is more… much more to know about Heaven.

We could go on and on in our study and would have only begun to scratch the surface. What we have been seeking to do is to simply begin to delve deeply into some things that matter most. Sometimes, we spend far too much time in that which matters less and not more. The good news is that we have time ahead when we can keep on learning.

Someone may object saying, "But what if we die?"

If we have made our commitment to Jesus and Jesus alone for our reception of the free gift of salvation that He purchased for us on the Cross of Calvary, death is not the end. In fact, unless Jesus our Lord and Savior returns before that time, we will need to die so that we can take the next step in life.

For now, all the learning will only be "in part." But, when we get to Heaven, we will know "in full."

After Columbus discovered the new world, Spain minted coins with the Latin slogan *Plus Ultra* that meant "More Beyond."[84] At that time we are told there were many who believed that the earth was flat and not round.

Their mental horizons needed expanding.

---

[84] Randy Alcorn uses this analogy in his book *50 Days of Heaven*. See page 255.

Hopefully, through the study of Heaven we have begun to experience expanded horizons, in many ways. Our thinking, our understanding, our application of God's inspired Word, and our commitments to more serious study and followship as disciples of Christ should be impacted.

I would be remiss to not acknowledge that some people will miss all these blessings.

Notice Revelation 21:7-8,25-27, 22:14-15—

> Those who are victorious will inherit all this, and I will be their God and they will be my children. But the cowardly, the unbelieving, the vile, the murderers, the sexually immoral, those who practice magic arts, the idolaters and all liars—they will be consigned to the fiery lake of burning sulfur.  This is the second death...

> On no day will its gates ever be shut, for there will be no night there. The glory and honor of the nations will be brought into it. Nothing impure will ever enter it, nor will anyone who does what is shameful or deceitful, but only those whose names are written in the Lamb's book of life.

> Blessed are those who wash their robes, that they may have the right to the tree of life and may go through the gates into the city. Outside are the dogs, those who practice magic arts, the sexually immoral, the murderers, the idolaters and everyone who loves and practices falsehood.

We must share the message of total redemption available now through Jesus Christ alone. His invitation is clearly stated in Revelation 22:16-17—

> "I, Jesus, have sent my angel to give you this testimony for the churches. I am the Root and the Offspring of David, and the bright Morning Star."

> The Spirit and the bride say, "Come!"

> And let the one who hears say, "Come!"

> Let the one who is thirsty come; and let the one who wishes take the free gift of the water of life.

# Teaching Outline

*The following outline is provided to assist you in teaching or reviewing the material. You'll find the title of each chapter, followed by the main idea, the main points (A-B-C-), and the sub-points (1-2-3-).*

## Part 1 — What is Heaven?

### 1. Being Heavenly-Minded is Earthly Good

*Main idea: The destination you plan to reach informs your journey— including how you plan and prepare during the days leading to your arrival. Likewise, being heavenly-minded is earthly good.*

A. Planning the journey for a place you have never been

1. *Have we actually neglected to carefully consider what the Bible says about Heaven, our ultimate destination?*

2. *What do you personally believe about Heaven?*

3. *Why do you think there has there been so much neglect regarding teaching and learning about Heaven?*

B. Look up!

C. Four earthly benefits of being Heavenly-minded

1. *Focusing on Heaven reminds us of the brevity of our earthly life.*

2. *Focusing on Heaven prepares us for the certainty of judgment.*

3. *Focusing on Heaven motivates us to live pure lives.*

4. *Focusing on Heaven places suffering in perspective.*

E. How, then, should we prepare?

1. *Be sincerely grateful for our Heavenly citizenship.*

2. *Focus our thinking on the things above to develop an eternal perspective.*

3. *Remember we are pressing forward toward the prize prepared for us.*

## 2. The Difference in Heaven Now & Heaven in the Future

*Main idea: The present Heaven provides us a glimpse of the future Heaven. The present Heaven is where believers go when they die— and is the sacred place many have seen.*

A. According to theologians the Bible actually refers to multiple "heavens."

1. *The 1st heaven is Earth's atmosphere.*

2. *The 2nd heaven is what we usually call outer space.*

3. *The 3rd Heaven points to the place where God dwells.*

4. *The 4th Heaven refers to a future Heaven that God is preparing for us even now.*

B. Understanding the present Heaven and the future Heaven

1. *Elisha saw Elijah go up into Heaven by a whirlwind.*

2. *Isaiah saw the Lord on His throne.*

3. *Ezekiel saw visions of God in the Heavenly throne room.*

4. *Nebuchadnezzar saw visions of Heaven.*

5. *Daniel saw into Heaven in the night visions.*

6. *Stephen saw Jesus Standing at the right hand of God.*

7. *Paul heard Jesus speaking to him from Heaven.*

8. *Peter talked with the Lord.*

9. *John saw an angel and heard a great multitude from Heaven.*

10. *Jesus told Nathanael that he would see Heaven opened.*

11. *Jesus saw the Heavens opened and the Spirit of God descending.*

C. Where do believers in Jesus Christ go when they die?

D. Is the "Present Heaven" a physical place?

E. How we might understand it— a helpful "parable."

## 3. The Essence of Eternal Life

*Main idea: Jesus defined eternal life as "knowing God." In Heaven we will be fully present with all of God, yet we will also continue receiving unfolding revelation of His goodness and glory.*

A. Knowing God

B. The "beatific vision"… three Latin words… "a happy-making sight"

1. *God, who is transcendent, became immanent and fully present when Jesus came to Earth as Immanuel— "God with us."*

2. *When we see Jesus in Heaven, we will see God to an even greater degree than we saw Him before.*

C. God— the Almighty Creator, Redeemer, Sustainer, Savior, and Lord— is our Father who is in Heaven.

1. *Not only do we long to be with God, but God has declared His intention for intimate relationship with us.*

2. *God— and relationship with Him— will be the center around which Heaven revolves.*

3. *God's glory won't be isolated to one place in Heaven, however. He will "fill" all of it.*

4. *We will never know all there is to know about God. We will never tire of learning more about Him.*

D. Heaven will mean we will be totally with "all" of God— the complete Trinity.

1. *We will be with God the Father— just as Jesus promised in John 14:6.*

2. *We will be with Jesus the Son, who also promised He would be there (John 14:2-4).*

3. *We will be with the Holy Spirit.*

E. Lessons from Luke 12:37, Matthew 20:28, John 13:8, and Isaiah 25:6.

F. Three ways we will worship God.

1. *We will learn to focus on the Beatific Vision without distraction.*

2. *We will worship God in an all-encompassing way.*

3. *Worship will not and cannot be boring or draining— it will be stirring, captivating, and motivating.*

G. How may/must people prepare for Heaven— our journey there and entry in?

# Part 2 — Truths to Think About More Often

## 4. Why the Resurrection Means So Much

*Main idea: When Jesus arose from the dead 2,000 years ago, we arose with Him. Furthermore, He became the first fruits of the New Creation, showing what we're destined to become.*

A. Redemption is physical as well as spiritual— God restores all things.

1. *Jesus' Resurrection is the model for mankind.*

2. *Jesus' Resurrection is the gateway for all of Creation.*

3. *Jesus' Resurrection will be our reality, too!*

B. What will our resurrected bodies be like?

1. *Jesus' resurrected life is the model for our new bodies.*

2. *We will have intermediate, temporary bodies in the "present Heaven."*

3. *There will be critical continuity between our bodies now and then.*

4. *Our final bodies will be like Christ's.*

5. *We will have a real physical / spiritual body.*

6. *We will have a recognizable body and a familiar voice.*

7. *We will have an imperishable body.*

8. *We will have a glorified body.*

9. *We will have a strong body.*

10. *We will have a body without limitations.*

*11. We will have an eternal body.*

## 5. Our Role in Ruling with Christ

*Main idea: From the beginning of time, we discover that we were created for relationship and rulership. Although the Fall postponed our potential, it didn't eliminate— or change— it.*

A. Why God created mankind and the earth and the universe— back to the beginning

   *1. We were designed to rule / reign.*

   *2. We were designed for relationship.*

B. The Fall— and the fix.

   *1. The roles of Adam and Eve = ruling the earth for the glory of God.*

   *2. Redemption— and Heaven— reveal a restoration of mankind's position, role, and responsibility.*

C. The outcome: a fully-restored relationship and a reinstatement of our role.

   *1. The glory in which God resides, God also provides.*

   *2. The position and the promises revealed in Revelation.*

D. The Throne reveals much about our relationship with God.

   *1. The Kingdom transfer startles the imagination— and it is coming.*

   *2. Reigning in the future is a reward of service and the inheritance for faithfulness now.*

   *3. Along with thrones, crowns are the primary Biblical indicators of ruling.*

## 6. Understanding the Millennium

*Main idea: Though there is some disagreement as to when the reign occurs and whether the 1,000 years is symbolic or literal, we can all agree: Jesus returns and reigns. Moreover, we will see a radical difference between His first coming and His return.*

A. Three views on the Millennium

   1. *Postmillennial (Christ returns after the Millennium)*

   2. *Amillennial (with the prefix a—, meaning "without," or "no" Millennium)*

   3. *Premillennial (Christ returns before the Millennium)*

B. Three truths to remember about each of these views.

   1. *They are each based on Scripture— on the same passage.*

   2. *The difference in interpretation centers on when we reign with Christ, that is, how we view Revelation 20:7—*

   3. *Our approach to the Millennium does not need to affect our view of the New Heaven and the New Earth.*

C. A call for humility

D. Four purposes of the Millennium

   1. *The Millennium will be a reward for the people of God.*

   2. *The Millennium will be a time of fulfillment of the prophetic pronouncements.*

   3. *The Millennium will provide the answer to the Model Prayer.*

   4. *The Millennium will provide a demonstration of a better world still incomplete.*

E. What to expect during the Millennium

   1. *A time of peace will be experienced.*

   2. *Prosperity will be realized abundantly.*

   3. *Purity will be the norm of life.*

   4. *Lifespans will be prolonged.*

   5. *Personal joy and contentment will be experienced in an era of happiness.*

F. Comparing His first coming (with some rejection) with His return (and His reign)

# Part 3 — What Will Heaven Be Like?

## 7. The Old Passes (the New Heaven and the New Earth)

*Main idea: A New Heaven and a New Earth are coming— they're promised. Before they can arrive, though, the present Earth must pass.*

A. Start with what's clear.

1. *We know that something new is coming— a new heaven and a new earth.*

2. *The old must pass away in order for the new to come.*

3. *This leads us to an obvious question: when will the fulfillment of this promise occur? When does the "new come" and the "old pass"?*

4. *Below we will evaluate the new that is coming— at the of this lesson and more in-depth in the following lesson— let's begin with what is passing.*

B. What does the Scripture mean that "heaven and earth will pass away"?

1. *What we see in the flood in Noah's day (2 Peter 3:5-7)*

2. *What we see in the resurrection of the body (1 Corinthians 15)*

3. *What we see in victory over death (1 Corinthians 15)*

4. *What we see from words and phrases featured throughout these passages.*

C. The principles of the New Heaven and the New Earth— what's coming.

1. *The removal of the sea = no more separation between people and groups.*

2. *The reversal of the curse of the Fall = no more causes of pain, no reminders of it.*

3. *Notably, everything is restored in the New Heaven and New Earth.*

D. A supernatural encounter— that's both an ending and a new beginning

## 8. The New Comes (the New Heaven and the New Earth)

*Main idea: Scripture describes the New Heaven and New Earth— what is coming — as both a country and a city. This is the place of our true citizenship.*

A. Two terms help us comprehend Heaven

1. *Scripture describes Heaven as a country.*
2. *Scripture describes Heaven as a city.*

B. God's country / nation / kingdom

1. *The glory of God will fill the earth.*
2. *The New Earth will be like Eden.*
3. *The Tree of Life will be on Earth.*
4. *The River of Life will flow forever.*
5. *The deserts will gush with water.*
6. *A beautiful and bountiful land will flourish.*
7. *Animals will be plentiful and peaceful.*

C. The Holy City, the New Jerusalem— the "city of cities"

1. *The City is massive.*
2. *The twelve gates of pearl, opening to the vast, high, broad wall.*
3. *The foundations, whose Architect and Builder is God.*
4. *Streets constructed of gold.*
5. *The Tree of Life.*
6. *The pure river of the water of life.*
7. *The main characteristic of this City is Holiness.*

D. The most important feature of all, the Presence.

## 9. Life in Heaven

*Main idea: Heaven is our permanent home. And, though questions abound, we can take comfort in the fact that God is completely good and He has prepared Heaven with us in mind.*

A. Our permanent, eternal dwelling place

  1. *Jesus is preparing a permanent home for us.*

  2. *The doctrine of the Resurrection indicates that we will be physical / spiritual beings living in an actual physical universe (as we previously studied).*

B. Eighteen common questions about Heaven— and our best attempts to answer them

  1. *Will the New Heaven and New Earth have a sun, a moon, oceans, and weather?*

  2. *Will we be ourselves or might we lose ourselves?*

  3. *Will we become angels?*

  4. *Will we have emotions and desires?*

  5. *Will we still have our unique personal identities?*

  6. *What will our bodies be like?*

  7. *Will we all be extremely beautiful?*

  8. *What age will we be?*

  9. *Will we have our same five senses?*

  10. *Will we have new abilities?*

  11. *Will we be male and female?*

  12. *Will we wear clothes?*

  13. *What will we eat and drink— if we eat and drink?*

  14. *Will we get hungry and will we digest food?*

  15. *Will we be capable of committing sin?*

  16. *Will we be tempted to sin and if so, will we have free will?*

  17. *Will we be truly perfect?*

  18. *Will we know everything?*

C. You will fully enjoy Heaven

# Part 4 — What Will We Do?

## 10. Destined for Deeper Relationships

*Main idea: God is relational, and we're created in His image. We were, therefore, designed for relationship— with Him and with others. In Heaven this won't be lessened; it will be amplified.*

   A. Will we need relationships in addition to our relationship with God in Heaven?

      1. *God's Word is clear that if we love God, we will also love people.*

      2. *Heaven will not eradicate the ways in which we express love. Rather, Heaven will enhance how we love.*

   B. How we will relate to ourselves

      1. *We will retain our identities and personalities.*

      2. *We will be given a "new name."*

      3. *We will retain our ethnic identities.*

      4. *We will have perfect bodies— without faults or infirmities.*

      5. *We will not remember things which bring sorrow or sadness… or, at least, we will understand them in a new way.*

   C. How we will relate to others

      1. *We will be reunited with our families and friends.*

      2. *We will know each other even better and more completely.*

      3. *We will love each other more deeply, in a greater dimension— and, as result, experience true community / koinonia.*

      4. *Marriage will (likely) change, yet we must remember that God always "trades up" in His plan of redemption.*

      5. *Will sexuality exist in Heaven?*

   D. How we will relate to God

      1. *We will see Him— and we will know Him.*

      2. *We will also be like Him.*

      3. *We will have close association with Jesus the Son and with God the Father.*

4. *We will worship and marvel.*

# 11. Managing the Misconceptions and Clarifying Expectations

*Main idea: Since we study Heaven so little, misconceptions abound. However, Heaven will be the most fulfilling experience— and it won't end. In fact, it will continue getting better and better the longer it lasts.*

A. Three misconceptions about Heaven

1. *Misconception #1 = God is a cosmic killjoy.*
2. *Misconception #2 = Heaven will be monotonous, routine, and boring.*
3. *Misconception #3 = Heaven will be one long church service.*

B. If not that, then what…?

1. *Joy and Happiness await in Heaven.*
2. *Restored health awaits us, as well.*
3. *Prosperity and security are available to everyone in Heaven.*
4. *Peace and safety will be unfailing.*
5. *We will not feel sad, cry, mourn, or face death.*
6. *We will recognize and relate to each other.*
7. *Our resurrected bodies will be locked into an appropriate age.*
8. *Our perception of family members will be uniquely appropriate.*
9. *We will work… and it will be fulfilling.*
10. *We will be playful and active.*
11. *We will have individual dwellings (homes).*
12. *We will enjoy fellowship meals, banquets, significant feasts, and special suppers.*

C. Always growing and learning and experiencing more

D. Rest, refreshment, rejuvenation…

# 12. Worship as a Way of Life— Then and Now

*Main idea: Worship will be our way of life in Heaven (our definition of worship is far too narrow). We began our study learning about how to plan for our ultimate destination. One of the best ways to prepare is to live now in the same way we'll live then— with worship as our way of life, living the prayer "on earth as it is in Heaven."*

A. A glimpse into the future

B. Will we be involved in one long worship event?

C. The throne remains the center.

1. *Many scholars regard Revelation 4 and Revelation 5 as the greatest exposition on the subject of worship found in the Bible.*

2. *Revelation 4:2-3 indicates the key word of these verses to be a word repeated 42 times in Revelation, throne. Everything flows from the throne.*

3. *The heavenly throne of God testifies to His sovereignty, authority, reign, and His absolute power over all.*

4. *In Revelation 5 the scene expands to include not only God the Father but God the Son.*

5. *There seems to be a growing crescendo with a steady increase in volume and strength.*

6. *What is revealed in John's experience regarding the contrast of present Earth and Heaven?*

D. Four worship principles revealed in God's Word

1. *Worship is not about us; worship is about God.*

2. *Worship is not so much about here as it is about there.*

3. *Worship helps us to realize that our "now" is not as important as our "then."*

4. *Worship should be both private and public.*

# Bibliography

Alcorn, Randy. *Heaven*. Wheaton, IL: Tyndale, 2004

Alcorn, Randy. *Heaven, Biblical Answers to Common Questions*. Wheaton, IL : Tyndale, 2004

Alcorn, Randy. *50 Days of Heaven*. Wheaton, ILL: Tyndale, 2006

Demy, Timothy and Ice, Thomas. *The End Times*. Grand Rapids, MI: Kregel, 2011

Enns, Paul. *Heaven Revealed*. Chicago, ILL: Moody, 2011

Graham, Billy. *The Heaven Answer Book*. Nashville, TN: Nelson, 2012

Hitchcock, Mark. *101 Answers – End Times*. Colorado Springs, CO: Multnomah, 2001

Lutzer, Erwin. *Spend Eternity with God*. Chicago, ILL: Moody, 1996

Lutzer, Erwin. *One Minute After You Die*. Chicago, ILL: Moody, 1997

Lutzer, Erwin. *Your Eternal Reward*. Chicago, ILL: Moody, 1998

Jeffress, Robert. *A Place Called Heaven*. Grand Rapids, MI: Baker, 2017

Jeremiah, David. *The Book of Signs*. Nashville, TN: Nelson, 2019

MacArthur, John. *Revelation 12-22. The MacArthur New Testament Commentary*. Chicago, IL: Moody, 2000

Washington, Linda. Compiler. *Everything the Bible Says About Heaven*. Bloomington, MN: Bethany House, 2011

# About the Author

Brother Edwin (or simply Edwin)— either of which he prefers being addressed— delights in his family. He married the love of his life, Joan, in 1969. Edwin and Joan have two sons, Andrew Edwin and Matthew Russell, and one daughter, Amanda Elyese. In addition, their lives have been bountifully blessed with twelve biological grandchildren, two adopted grandchildren, and three step-grandchildren. He says that instead of a family tree, he and Joan have become grateful patron and matron of a small orchard.

Edwin F. Jenkins has been involved in ministry for more than 53 years. Born in Birmingham, Alabama he was converted and called into ministry as a member of the Boyles Baptist Church in Tarrant, Alabama. He was licensed and ordained to Gospel Ministry by First Baptist Church of Trussville, Alabama and Lone Willow Baptist Church, Cleburne, Texas respectively.

He has served churches in Alabama and Texas as Minister of Youth, Associate Pastor, and Pastor. In addition, he has taught on adjunct faculty for New Orleans Baptist Theological Seminary, Jeff State Community College, and Samford University Ministry Training Institute. For nearly ten years he served as State Missionary of the Alabama Baptist Convention State Board of Missions.

Brother Edwin graduated from Samford University with a Bachelor of Arts and from Southwestern Baptist Theological Seminary in Fort Worth Texas with Master of Divinity and Doctor of Ministry degrees.

**Special Thanks**

Grateful appreciation is expressed to Andrew Edwin Jenkins for his extremely beneficial expertise and helpfulness in bringing this publication into reality.

Andrew, an author of more than twenty books as a Christian writer, also has extensive experience serving as a Minister, Pastor, Facilitator, and Leader of non-profit endeavors— and as an expert Consultant and Organizer for several Christian enterprises. Without his assistance and encouragement this project would not have come to fruition.

He may be contacted through his websites…

- www.Jenkins.tv

- www.AmplifyOnline.info

… or directly by email or phone.

- andy@Jenkins.tv

- 205-291-1391


**Additional expression of gratitude from the author—**

Joan Evans Jenkins provided outstanding assistance and exhibited patient endurance and demonstrated all aspects of the Fruit of the Spirit throughout the various stages of development of this book. Huge "thank you"s and hugs are extended to Joan for all she is, all she does, and all she will continue to do in the many projects upon which Edwin and Joan embark, always together.

Made in the USA
Columbia, SC
29 September 2024

43205361R00161